# Chamber of Nothing

## Cathy Forde

**Non-fiction section by Christopher Edge**

www.pearsonschoolsandfecolleges.co.uk

✓ Free online support
✓ Useful weblinks
✓ 24 hour online ordering

0845 630 33 33

Heinemann

Part of Pearson

Heinemann is an imprint of Pearson Education Limited, Edinburgh Gate, Harlow, Essex, CM20 2JE.

www.pearsonschoolsandfecolleges.co.uk

Heinemann is a registered trademark of Pearson Education Limited

Text © Cathy Forde 2011
Non-fiction text © Christopher Edge 2011
Typeset by Kamae Design
Cover design by Craft Design
Cover photo © asliuzunoglu/Shutterstock and Dgmata/Shutterstock

The rights of Cathy Forde and Christopher Edge to be identified as authors of this work have been asserted by them in accordance with the Copyright, Designs and Patents Act 1988.

First published 2011

14 13 12 11 10
10 9 8 7 6 5 4 3 2 1

**British Library Cataloguing in Publication Data**
A catalogue record for this book is available from the British Library

ISBN 978 0 435 04607 1

Printed by Henry Ling, UK

*To Ellen.*

*If you hadn't invited me along that stange, strange night,
I would never have written this play.*

# Contents

# Cast list

## MILTON STREET PUPILS

**DEZ** (Desmond) – Always asking questions. Mainly pointless ones.

**DONZ (DONNA)** Annoying but completely harmless. A pest.

**GABZ (GABRIELLE)** Sharp and mouthy. Tricky to impress.

**JACKY (JACQUELINE)** Gabz's boy-crazy best pal. Equally sharp and mouthy.

**LEE (McGEE)** Curious, bright, asthmatic. His own person regardless of teasing.

**MEL (MELANIE)** Sensitive and nervy.

**NAT (NATALIE)** Jumpy and needy.

**SAM SULLIVAN (SULLY)** A handful. Cocky and bold.

**JOE (JOSEPH MORRISON)** Sam's sidekick. Plenty of mouth but not a lot of bottle.

**TONE (ANTHONY)** Not the brightest torch in the tunnel.

## MILTON STREET TEACHERS

**MRS MORAG PRESLEY** (aka 'ELVIS') – The teacher in charge. Ground down and jaded. Permanently exasperated. Nothing can impress her.

**MR RUPERT YOUNG** Quite new to teaching. A gentleman. Not a bad bone in his body. Very enthusiastic and positive.

## OTHER ADULTS

**BOB THE DRIVER** Sarcastic bus driver.

**GORDON** Official Hidden City Tour Guide.

**THE GUIDE** Female. A blank canvas.

# Notes from the author

1. This play is an ensemble piece with fifteen characters, most of them involved in almost every scene and given plenty to say. I wrote my play this way because I have memories, both as a pupil and a teacher, of 'doing' plays in class where only a few pupils had speaking parts. Non-cast members would sit bored and disengaged during the reading, and those with small roles spent their drama time hung up on reading their one or two lines and not following the rest of the play. That's no fun. From the start, I want the whole cast to enjoy being part of this play and to feel important to it.

   Although I have created specific speaking parts for ten pupils and two teachers, in a bigger class other actors could easily be cast in non-speaking parts, bulking out the tour group as pupils, or even playing extra adult helpers, crowding into the chambers and reacting to different scenes as they unfold. Such additional cast members can even create their own dialogue in the 'improv' sections. (See note 4 below.)

2. This play works as both as a 'static' classroom text (i.e. read in a class with all pupils sitting at their desks, imagining the action) and a physical piece of theatre that could be performed to an audience. No set is required, and the only props needed are a few torches and mobile phones. I like the idea of a cast and crew devising their own set, deciding how each chamber might look and playing with light and shadows. I have deliberately avoided suggesting sound effects. Given the setting, there are many creative sonic opportunities throughout, and again I like the idea of different casts and crews creating their own unique 'soundtrack' from the text.

3. To make the dialogue come over as naturally as possible, there have to be many occasions where characters talk at once, interrupting and overlapping each other. Wherever a backslash (/) appears at the end and beginning of lines, there should be an overlap in chat. An en-dash – at the end of the line indicates interrupted speech, where the next speaker cuts off the current speaker.

4. There are various points throughout the play where the characters all talk at once in reaction to something that has happened. Although I have written specific dialogue in these sections, I hope that some casts might grow to feel they 'know' their characters well enough to improvise their own dialogue. Directors, teachers and drama leaders can therefore opt to ignore the text of the play and improvise at these points, which are marked with an asterisk (*).

5. I don't want to reveal too much about the Guide before anyone meets her in the play, but let's just say she is a strange woman. It is important that the distinct spirit of each chamber, and the characters and stories associated with it, affect her mood and behaviour, so you never quite get a handle on her true identity.

6. Enough notes.

On with the show …

# Scene One

## The Coach Journey

*Pupils are seated on a coach for a school outing and a boistrous carry-on is in full swing, complete with raucous communal singing. This includes a tentative Mr Young, but definitely, definitely not Mrs Presley.*

**PUPILS AND MR YOUNG** (*singing*) *Stop the bus I need a wee-wee, Stop the bus I need a wee-wee, Stop the bus I need a wee-wee … /*

**NAT** /(*squirming*) Everyone lay off singing that/

**PUPILS AND MR YOUNG** /*I need to go right now!*                                      5

**JOE** (*conducting*) All together now! A-one, two, three – /

**MRS PRESLEY** /Down off the seat, Joseph Morrison! You've been told twice already/

**PUPILS AND MR YOUNG** /*Stop the bus I need a wee-wee, Stop the bus I*     10
*need a wee-wee … /*

**MRS PRESLEY** /Off that seat this instant, I said!/

**PUPILS AND MR YOUNG** /*Stop the bus I need a wee-wee … /*

**MRS PRESLEY** /And do not even *think* about opening that emergency door again, Sam Sullivan.          15

**SAM** But what if we're in a smash, Miss? And the front of the bus is all mega-mangled up, Miss?

**JOE** (*sings*) *The front of the bus is mangled up, mangled up, mangled up … /*

**MEL** /Ey! Quit, you! That's totally tempting fate. 20

**SAM** And it's the only way to escape, Miss? And you might be bleeding out, Miss?

**JOE** Spurting. *Plaaahh!*

**SAM** I'd have to open it then, Miss. Else you might –

**MRS PRESLEY** *Sam!* 25

**SAM** Yes, Mrs Pres-ley. (*sings like Elvis*) *Or I'll wet my blue suede shoes.*

**MR YOUNG** (*impressed by impression*) Oh, I say!

**JOE** And again … All together now!

**DEZ** Are we there yet?/ 30

**PUPILS** /*Stop the bus I need a wee-wee …/*

*The chanting carries on in the background as the following characters speak.*

**NAT** /Oooh, please quit. I'm totally bursting.

**JACKY** Tell you what, Nat. Keep up moaning in my ear and I'll be moving next to Sam.

**SAM** In your dreams. 35

**JOE** Your nightmares, matey.

**JACKY** I heard that.

**DONZ** Miss, Nat needs the toilet, Miss.

**SAM** C'mon! Sound effects everyone!

**JOE** A-one, two, three … 40

2

**PUPILS** *Pssssshhhh./*

**MRS PRESLEY** /Right, Milton Street. Settle!

**BOB THE DRIVER** (*grumbling to himself*) What a shower!

**PUPILS** *Stop the bus I need a wee-wee … (**the chanting
continues**)* 45

**NAT** I really, really do!

**LEE** Hey, that fits the song! (*sings*) *I really, really do.*

**GABZ** What you expect? Glugging that mega bottle
of fizzy?

**JACKY** All to your greedy pig self. 50

**DEZ** Sloshing about inside you now, is it? Eh? Eh?

**JOE** Blug, blug, bluuug.

**GABZ** Pr-e-e-e-ssing down on your bladder? Oooh, I
hate that feeling.

**DONZ** See Nat, Miss? Miss? She's bursting. Gonna 55
stop somewhere, Miss? Better, Miss. Before
she has an accident, Miss. All over the floor,
Miss.

**MRS PRESLEY** That's quite enough from you, Donna. And
drinking too much before a journey wasn't 60
very smart, Natalie, was it?

**JOE** She's not very smart.

**NAT** Thirsty, wasn't I?

**JACKY** Just munched away a family bag of salt 'n'
vinny to yourself, after all. 65

**GABZ** Guzzly guts. *Glug, glug, glug …*

**NAT** Stop –

3

**LEE** *– the bus I need a wee-wee. Haha, yeah, you know the song!* **(sniggers and then wheezes, short of breath)** 70

**TONE** Hur, hur, hur. Clever.

**SAM** **(sarcastic handclapping and pretend wheezing)** Aw, Lee, man. Better watch out you don't wheeze yourself dead at your own genius joke. 75

**MRS PRESLEY** Please don't tell me you forgot your inhaler again, Lee.

**LEE** Ooops.

**DONZ** Miss, Lee's forgot his inhaler, Miss.

**MRS PRESLEY** Well, if you get breathless underground, don't 80 come running to me.

**MEL** Underground?

**SAM** Lee run? No danger.

**LEE** I'll be fine, Miss.

**MEL** Nat won't. 85

**DONZ** Shoulda made us all go wee-wee, Miss, before we took the bus.

**MRS PRESLEY** I did. But do any of you ever listen, Milton Street?

**SAM** Someone speaking? 90

**DEZ** Where?

**JOE** I don't hear anything.

**DONZ** Shoulda forced us, Miss. You're in charge, Miss.

**MRS PRESLEY** Thank you, Donna. And since we're on the subject of who's in charge, and we're almost there – (*claps for attention*) 95

**DEZ** Are we there yet?

**MRS PRESLEY** Everyone! (*pauses to look around at the pupils*) Sam, away from the emergency door, I said.

**SAM** (*Elvis voice*) Yes, ma'am. 100

**MRS PRESLEY** Please remember that Mr Young and I –

**PUPILS** Oooooh-eeee-oooooh!

**DONZ** Are gettin' married, Miss? Ooooh! Can I be bridesmaid, Miss?

**MRS PRESLEY** – are in charge of you, just like at school – 105

**SAM** (*aside to Gabz, Joe and Mel*) Youngy-Dung's never in charge of the Milton Street Massive.

**GABZ** Tries his tweedy-weedy best.

**JOE** But he's so not.

**MEL** Not even in charge of his side parting. 110

**GABZ** Squigglering all over his scalp, innit?

**MRS PRESLEY** – and although you are out of uniform this evening –

**MR YOUNG** Ahem, and looking terrifically à la mode, I must say. 115

**TONE** Huh?

**SAM** Suited, Youngy's saying.

**JOE** Booted.

**GABZ** Check it, yeah. Dudes-in-the-hoodies all dressed up Dapper Dan. 120

**MRS PRESLEY** – you are still ambassadors for Milton Street School.

**TONE** Ambassa … Huh?

**JACKY** Brand-new gear all round. Am I right, Supadry guy? 12

**JOE** Nuh-uh.

**JACKY** Your mummykins take you out shopping, did she?

**GABZ** Hold your little handy?

**JOE AND SAM** Nuh-uh! 13

**JACKY** Coulda asked me down the mall any day, Sam. I woulda picked ya out something to match your eyes.

**GABZ** What? Bloodshot and squinty?

**JACKY** (*smiling and fluttering her eyelashes at Sam*) Baby 13 blue.

**JOE** (*aside to Sam*) Lucky escape there, mate.

**MEL** By the way, Sam, what's with all the crazy-boy hair-gel action?

**GABZ** Yeah, talk us through your style there, Sully. 14

**JACKY** Spiked yourself up into little perfect peaks, haven't you?

**SAM** Eh? No!

**GABZ** Eh, yeah. Like the top of a lemon meringue pie. (*pats Sam's hair*) Oooh, prickly too. Like a 14 cute little baby hedgehog –

**SAM** Oi! Don't touch what you can't afford, girl.

**GABZ** What? When we're down the pound shop?

*All at once the other girls speak.*

*****JACKY** Good one, girlfriend!

*****MEL** Good one! 150

*****NAT** Miii-*aow*!

*****DONZ** Pound shop, Miss. You hear that?

**SAM** What does that even mean?

**TONE** Pound shop?

**LEE** Think she's saying, like, you're something to 155
buy.

**TONE** Aha. In a shop –

**LEE** Yeah.

**MEL** – you'd be cheap an' nasty. Like Samster.

**GABZ** Gold star! 160

**SAM** Me? Cheap? Chuh!

**NAT** Miss, I'm in agony, Miss!/

**SAM** /(*sings over Nat*) Before I wet the seat.

**ALL BOYS** Too late! (*they start to sing*) *Stop the bus I need a
wee-wee …* (*carry on chanting*) 165

**MRS PRESLEY** (*clapping for attention*) So, Milton Street pupils.

**SAM** M. Street Massive. Yo! Yo! Listen up. Da King
speaks.

**MRS PRESLEY** I expect nothing less than best behaviour
tonight – 170

*General groan from pupils.*

**MRS PRESLEY** And by best behaviour, what do I mean?
Joseph?

7

JOE  I dunno, do I?

MRS PRESLEY  Anyone?

DONZ  Miss! MISS!

MRS PRESLEY  Anyone?

DONZ  (*waving her hand*) *MISS!*

MRS PRESLEY  No? Well, if no one can even tell me what they think best behaviour is, let alone put it into practice, I'd better tell our driver –

BOB THE DRIVER  Name's Bob.

*All the pupils respond together.*

*LEE  Hello, Mr Bob.

*DONZ  Yeah, hello, Mr Bob.

*DEZ  Rob?

*TONE  Rob who?

*JACKY  Hiya, Bobby. I'm Jacky.

*GABZ  Ignore her.

*SAM  Yo, dude.

*JOE  Ey up, Bob.

*MEL  Hi there.

*NAT  Are we nearly there, Bob?

BOB THE DRIVER  I'll Bob the lot of you.

MRS PRESLEY  Settle! I just have to tell Bob to drive us straight back to Milton Str–/

SAM  /Miss! I know what best behaviour is! No fighting.

JOE  And no swearing.

**MRS PRESLEY** Better. Anyone else?

**GABZ** (*aside*) Why's Elvis totally eyeballing me like
that? Like I look like someone who knows           200
anything about 'best behaviour'.

**MRS PRESLEY** Is that you saying you want Bob to take us
back, Gabrielle?

**GABZ** No backchat, Miss.

**MRS PRESLEY** Good. Jacqueline?           205

**JACKY** Er. No smoking?

**MRS PRESLEY** I should think not, Milton Street!

**MEL** Ya don't even smoke, Jacky.

**JACKY** So? Would count as bad behaviour if I did.

**LEE** Bad habit, not behaviour.           210

**DONZ** Miss!

**MRS PRESLEY** Anyone else? Anthony?

**TONE** Em, er … I've to be on my best … .

*General snoring noises from pupils.*

**LEE** No pushing. Cos that's dangerous.

**GABZ, JACKY,
MEL, SAM
AND JOE** Yeah, *dangerous*.           215

**LEE** It is! Down stairs and that. Joe's always trying
to push me down stairs.

**MRS PRESLEY** Well, he'd better not tonight. Of course it's
dangerous. Good, Lee.

**JOE** (*mimicking Mrs Presley*) Good, Lee.           220

**LEE** Cheers, Joe!

**MRS PRESLEY** Anything else?

9

**BOB THE DRIVER** (*aside to Mr Young*) Rather you than me policing this shower, mate.

**MR YOUNG** Sorry? Shower?

**MEL** (*to Mrs Presley*) Is no scratching good?

**BOYS** Scratching?

**TONE** It's the business when you're itchy.

**SAM** Brainshare.

**MEL** I mean scratching someone *back*.

***DEZ** Scratching someone's *back*?

***DONZ** No thanks!

***LEE** Sick!

***NAT** Yuck!

***GABZ** Gross!

**JACKY** Only if it's a spot-free zone.

**SAM** Another brainshare.

**MEL** Scratching back at someone fighting you, stoopid. Clawing eyes out and that. *Meow*.

**TONE AND JACKY** Ahhh.

**MRS PRESLEY** Fighting of any description is never all right, Melanie.

**DEZ** What about boxing?

**MR YOUNG** Ah! Now that's a fighting *sport*.

**JACKY** Or pillow-fighting?

**GABZ** Yeah. That's not dangerous.

**LEE** Could be. Like if feathers fly down your windpipe.

**MRS PRESLEY AND TONE** Feathers?

**MR YOUNG** Now scratching would definitely come under 250
fighting in my book, Mrs Presley.

**MRS PRESLEY** Thank you, Mr Young.

**TONE** Itchy scratching?

**MRS PRESLEY** No, Anthony. That would be different from
clawing someone's eyes out. 255

**TONE** Phew. Cos I love a good scratch, me.

**GABZ** Too much information.

**MRS PRESLEY** But don't feel you have scratch all over for rest
of the night, just because it's allowed.

**TONE** I'll try. 260

**MRS PRESLEY** And just try to remember as far as tonight
goes, fighting of *any* description is bad
behaviour: pushing, scratching, punching –
Sam!

*Sam has Lee in a headlock.*

**LEE** Ow! 265

**SAM** We're just play-fighting, ain't we, Lee!

**LEE** Er, no. You're fighting fighting.

**MRS PRESLEY** Especially since we're going underground.

**DEZ** Eh?

**JOE** How deep underground? 270

**GABZ** Scared there, little Baby Joe-Joe?

**JACKY** I'll hold your handy if you like.

**JOE** I'm not that scared.

**MRS PRESLEY** And it could be dark.

**DEZ** Eh?

**MEL** I hate dark places.

**SAM AND LEE** Cooo-ell.

**DEZ** How dark?

**MEL** Don't fancy the sound of that either. Do I need to go, Miss?

**MRS PRESLEY** Yes.

**NAT** I hate the dark and all. Spooks me well out.

**MRS PRESLEY** Nonsense. Anyway, you'll all behave, yes?

*'Stop the bus' song starts up quietly.*

**MRS PRESLEY** (*louder*) I didn't hear a 'yes'.

**PUPILS** Yes!

**MRS PRESLEY** 'Yes' what? Are we forgetting something?

**DONZ** Nat forgot to go wee-wee.

**JOE** Tone forgot his brain.

**LEE** I forgot my inhaler.

**MRS PRESLEY** 'Yes, Mrs …'

**PUPILS** *Pres*-ley.

**MRS PRESLEY** And?

**PUPILS** And?/Huh?/What?/Duh?

**MRS PRESLEY** Aren't we forgetting who else is in charge? 'Yes, Mrs Presley and Mr …'

*Pupils all chime at once.*

**\*DONZ AND LEE** Young./

**\*JACKY AND GABZ** /Youngy-Young./

**\*SAM AND JOE** /Young-Dung-Bung./

| | | |
|---|---|---|
| **\*TONE** | /Old. | |
| **\*DEZ, DONZ AND NAT** | Old? | 300 |
| **MRS PRESLEY** | Better. You are very lucky, not only that Mr Young – | |
| **\*JACKY AND GABZ** | Youngy-Young./ | |
| **\*SAM** | /Young-Dung-Bung./ | |
| **\*JOE** | /Hung-Stung./ | 305 |
| **MRS PRESLEY** | /Settle! Mr Young and I were available to give up our Sunday evening – | |
| **JACKY** | Like either of you had to cancel snoggin' hot dates to be here or something./ | |
| **\*GABZ** | /(*low*) With Mr Potato Head and Princess Fiona's big sister. | 310 |
| **MRS PRESLEY** | I heard that, ladies. | |

*'Stop the bus' song repeats in the background.*

| | | |
|---|---|---|
| **MRS PRESLEY** | (*louder, trying to make herself heard*) Not only have Mr Young and I given up our evening to do this, but you're even luckier because you're the very first visitors to this new attraction. | 315 |
| **NAT** | Miss, does this new attraction have a toilet? | |
| **DONZ** | Nat's gonna wet herself, Miss. | |
| **BOB THE DRIVER** | None of your shower better wet anything on my bus. | 320 |
| **MR YOUNG** | (*to Bob*) Sorry, driver? Didn't quite catch … It's a touch noisy. | |
| **MRS PRESLEY** | So I need to trust you *all* to behave. Or else. | |
| **MR YOUNG** | (*to Bob*) What can you do? | |

**JOE** Or else what, Miss? 32

**SAM** (*aside to Joe*) Gonna leave one of your naughty boys underground, Elvis? I don't think so.

**BOB THE DRIVER** (*to Mr Young*) Muzzles, boot camp, National Service –

**MR YOUNG** (*to Bob*) Sorry, it's tricky to hear you above the – 33

**BOB THE DRIVER** Rabble?

**MRS PRESLEY** Settle!

**MR YOUNG** They're beside themselves coming on this trip.

**SAM** Ho. Sir? Tonight totally better not be boring.

**JOE** We'd plans. 33

**MR YOUNG** (*to Bob*) This particular group … Super bunch really, but they tend to be rather …

**BOB THE DRIVER** Challenging?

**MR YOUNG** Especially when it comes to …

**BOB THE DRIVER** Discipline and attitude? 34

**MR YOUNG** Between you and me, they're normally excluded from out-of-school activities.

**BOB THE DRIVER** You surprise me.

**MR YOUNG** So this outing's such a treat.

**JACKY** Am I the only one bored out my coconut already? 34

**MR YOUNG** And I must confess, although they're being somewhat …

**BOB THE DRIVER** Vocal?

**MR YOUNG** I'm rather enjoying the high spirits. Sing-a-long takes me back to my Boy Scout days. 35

Sound of sizzling sausages around the
campfire, dib, dib, dib, dob, dob, dob –

**BOB THE DRIVER** Personally, I'd enjoy the sound of hearing
myself think a bit more. Like while I'm driving   355
this big bus.

**DEZ** Oi, Mr Y? We there yet?

**SAM** Like Youngy's gonna know. Ask Elvis.

**BOB THE DRIVER** Yup. What a shower.

**MR YOUNG** Shower? That won't matter tonight.   360

**MRS PRESLEY** Just hold on for two more minutes, Natalie.

**JOE** Woo. Can't wait!

**JACKY** Just like Natalie.

**MR YOUNG** (*to Bob*) We'll be underground, you see.
Although I have brought my trusty anorak, of   365
course. Just in case.

**BOB THE DRIVER** Go on a lot of excursions then?

**MR YOUNG** Maritime and railway museums mainly.

**BOB THE DRIVER** (*aside*) On your own, I take it?

**MR YOUNG** And I don't usually have company. So it's quite   370
marvellous to share an outing with my own
pupils.

**BOB THE DRIVER** New to the job, are you, mate?

**MR YOUNG** As a matter of fact, Milton Street's my first
teaching appointment …   375

**BOB THE DRIVER** Lucky you.

**MR YOUNG** Very lucky. (*pause*) Although there've been
one or two –

| | |
|---|---|
| **BOB THE DRIVER** | Teething problems? |
| **MR YOUNG** | Just getting used to – |
| **BOB THE DRIVER** | Your little treasures. |
| **MR YOUNG** | Their sense of humour can sometimes be rather …/ |
| **MEL** | /I think Tone's chucking up. |
| **MR YOUNG** | And getting through lessons without – |
| **BOB THE DRIVER** | Incident? |
| **MR YOUNG** | – can be something of a … (*pause*) Still, finally getting a break from the chalk and talk. Marvellous! |
| **GABZ** | Miss, Tone's gonna puke. |
| **PUPILS** | Miss. Miss! |

*Tone is making gagging sounds.*

| | |
|---|---|
| **PUPILS** | Ugh! |
| **DONZ** | Lumpy thing came up out his mouth there, Miss. Saw it, Miss. |
| ***PUPILS** | Ugggggghhh! |
| **MR YOUNG** | (*to Bob*) Yes, it's going to be quite an adventure! |
| **MRS PRESLEY** | We're stopping. He can hold it in. |
| **BOB THE DRIVER** | Better flaming had. |
| **NAT** | Miss! |
| **MRS PRESLEY** | And so can you, Natalie. Anthony. We're here. |

*Coach stops and pupils all rush to the exit of the coach. Tone is making gagging sounds.*

| | |
|---|---|
| ***NAT** | Toilet! |

38

38

39

39

40

**16**

| | | |
|---|---|---|
| ***LEE** | Hurray! | |
| ***JOE** | Move it! | |
| ***SAM** | I'm first! | 405 |
| ***MEL** | Mind? That was my foot. | |
| ***JACKY** | Ladies first! | |
| ***DEZ** | Ladies? | |
| ***GABZ** | You watch it! | |
| ***DONZ** | Miss, I'm totally mad excited. | 410 |
| **MRS PRESLEY** | Settle. No stampede. I'd let Anthony off first, Gabrielle. Move the handbag. And then Mr Young. | |
| **GABZ** | He can move himself. | |
| **DONZ** | Ah. You feeling sick too, Sir? | 415 |
| **MRS PRESLEY** | I mean let him *off*, Donna. Manners! | |
| **MR YOUNG** | Oh, it's quite all right, they're just being … Ouch! | |
| **SAM AND JOE** | (*singing*) *Here we go, here we go, here we go …* | |
| **DONZ** | Miss. Well dark, innit? | 420 |
| **DEZ** | Sure this is the right place? | |
| **SAM** | Read the sign, dipstick: Hidden City Tours. | |
| **MRS PRESLEY** | Everyone off? Good. How about we thank our driver? | |
| ***MEL, DONZ AND LEE** | Thank you, Bob. | 425 |
| ***TONE** | *Oof!* (*still making gagging sounds but gives thumbs-up to Bob*) | |
| ***SAM** | Ta, Bob! | |

17

**\*JOE** Respect.

**\*JACKY** See you later, Mr Bob.

**\*GABZ** What you like, Jacky? 43

**\*NAT** Toilet!

**MRS PRESLEY** (*to Bob*) An hour and half back here?

**BOB THE DRIVER** Missing you already.

**MRS PRESLEY** Sorry?

**BOB THE DRIVER** Hour and a half back here. 43

**MRS PRESLEY** Thank you. (*to pupils*) This way, Milton Street. Down the alley.

**BOB THE DRIVER** Good luck. Rather you than me, Missus.

*Blackout.*

## Office of Hidden City Tours

*Virtual darkness. \* Pupils can be heard offstage (in the toilets making an unruly noise, water running, toilets flushing, Tone gagging, etc.).*

*The main door to the office is open and Mrs Presley is banging on a closed door inside the office, holding an old-looking mobile phone in one hand. There is a desk with various leaflets on it. Mr Young is groping about, pointlessly flicking light switches but no lights come on.*

**MR YOUNG** Morag, it really doesn't seem as if anyone's …

**MRS PRESLEY** The door was open, wasn't it, Rupert? Must be someone about.

**MR YOUNG** But there's no sign of life, Morag. (*pause*) I … I'm just wondering …  5

**MRS PRESLEY** Just wondering what? Spit it out, Rupert.

**MR YOUNG** Would there have been some –

**MRS PRESLEY** What? Mistake with my arrangements? No. I don't make mistakes, Rupert.

**MR YOUNG** Of course not, Morag. And I-I wasn't suggesting/  10

| | |
|---|---|
| **MRS PRESLEY** | /And this office emailed yesterday. Eight p.m. someone's meant to meet – |
| **MR YOUNG** | Well, it's deserted. No lights. |
| **MRS PRESLEY** | I can see that, Rupert, thank you. |
| **MR YOUNG** | And it's eight fifteen. |
| **MRS PRESLEY** | And I can tell the time, thank you, Rupert. |
| **MR YOUNG** | Of course you can, Morag. I'm … I'm only thinking … If no one arrives … soon. The pupils; they'll be so … |
| **MRS PRESLEY** | Rupert, that motley rabble in there are more than capable of creating their own entertainment. They always do … (*pause*) unfortunately. |

*Enter Sam and Joe, bound in toilet paper.*

| | |
|---|---|
| **MRS PRESLEY** | I rest my case. |
| **MR YOUNG** | Oh, I say. |
| **MRS PRESLEY** | Stop acting like clowns! Get straight back and strip that zombie nonsense off. |
| **JOE** | We're mummies, Miss, not clowns. |
| **SAM** | But it's spooky-wooky dark in there, Miss. |
| **JOE** | We didn't do this anyways, Miss. |
| **SAM** | Someone else wrapped us up, Miss. |
| **JOE** | That Lee McGee, Miss. |
| **MRS PRESLEY** | Don't be ridiculous! |
| **JOE** | Floor's all wet and slippy in there too, Miss. |
| **SAM** | That wasn't me, Miss. |
| **JOE** | Lee again, Miss. |

**SAM** Putting his naughty thumbs under the taps.

**JOE** Yeah. Making water squirt out.

**SAM** Totally everywhere, Miss. You should see it. 40

**JOE** We'd never do that, Miss.

**SAM** We told him to stop, Miss. He wouldn't.

**JOE** He's well bad, that Lee. You should go in there, Miss.

**SAM** Punish him. 45

**JOE** Smack his bot.

**MRS PRESLEY** Do you two want to go straight back on the bus?

**JOE** Bus is gone, Miss.

**SAM** And you just said go back in the toilets, Miss. 50
Strip the zombie nonsense off. See: I'm paying attention, Miss.

**JOE** What d'you want us to do, Miss?

**SAM** I'm confused, Miss.

**JOE** Please, Miss, are we still going on the tour, 55
Miss?

**SAM** Under the city, Miss?

**JOE** Cos it doesn't look like nobody's here, Miss.

**MRS PRESLEY** Anybody.

**SAM** What he said, Miss. 60

**MRS PRESLEY** You're worse than Donna in stereo, you pair.
Stop bleating at me, for heaven's sake!

**JOE** But is this it, Miss?

**SAM** Cos it's a big bin bag of rubbish if it is.

> *While Sam and Joe are winding up Mrs Presley,*
> *enter Jacky and Gabz, also bound in toilet paper.*

**GABZ** Snap-snaps! 65

**JACKY** Great minds think alike, eh, boys?

**MRS PRESLEY** Oh, for the love of … (*shouting out of the main office door*) Milton Street. Everyone! Out! Now!

> *Enter Mel, Dez, Lee and Donz.*

**MRS PRESLEY** Everyone, I said!

**LEE** Tone's still scrubbing off vom. 70

**MR YOUNG** Dear, dear.

**MRS PRESLEY** Delightful.

**DONZ** Nat's fixing her slap.

**DEZ** In the dark?

**MRS PRESLEY** What on earth is she wasting her time doing 75 that for?

**GABZ** That's what I said.

**JACKY** Me too.

> *Enter Nat. She scowls at Gabz and Jacky.*

**GABZ** Don't think she's actually speaking to us now.

**JACKY** Yeah! If looks could kill. 80

**MRS PRESLEY** Right, go back and get the toilet paper off.

**JACKY** (*to Gabz, Sam and Joe*) Thought she just told us to come out?

**SAM** Make your mind up, Elvis.

**MRS PRESLEY** I heard that, Sam Sullivan. 85

> *Sam, Joe, Gabz and Jacky exit to return to the*
> *toilets while everyone else crowds the office.*

**MRS PRESLEY** Settle! And who can let me use their mobile?

**DONZ** Miss, you said leave our phones behind.

**LEE** On the bus.

**MEL** On pain of death.

**NAT** Cos if we brought them we'd end up posting     90
junk on Facebook all night, Miss.

**MRS PRESLEY** I wouldn't say junk.

**TONE** Just did, Miss.

**NAT** And maddy-mental pictures.

**MRS PRESLEY** And I would not say maddy-ment–     95

*Pupils laugh at Mrs Presley until she hisses.*

**MRS PRESLEY** Settle!

**LEE** You said no phones. Even though my mum
says, 'Lee, you make sure you have yours at all
times.' For emergencies, like.

**GABZ** Duh. If you're in an emergency –     100

**SAM** Or lying dead.

**GABZ** Hardly going to be able to stupid phone
anyway. So what's the point of that?

**MRS PRESLEY** And if there is an emergency, we'd use my
phone.     105

**MEL** But you've just asked to use someone else's,
Miss.

**MRS PRESLEY** So no one has a phone?

**LEE** One in your hand, Miss.

**MRS PRESLEY** Thank you, Lee. I am aware of that.     110

23

LEE Oh, man! And it's a really, really, really ancient Nokia.

*Crows of sympathy and mockery from the pupils.*

*DONZ Oh, Miss.

*LEE I'd ask for an upgrade.

*DONZ That's a sin, stuck with that phone. 11

*NAT My granny's got a better phone than that!

*MEL No camera, even.

*DEZ How can you even hold it, Miss? Does it not weigh a ton?

MRS PRESLEY I can't seem to get a signal. 12

MEL No dissing, Miss, but it's rubbish old gadg, that's why.

DONZ Serious. Should get an upgrade, Miss. I wouldn't be seen dead holding that.

DEZ Maybe you forgot to charge it, Miss? 12

MRS PRESLEY Thank you, Dez. I don't forget things.

MEL Why d'you not just use Mr Young's?

MRS PRESLEY Mr Young doesn't actually have –

DEZ, LEE, MEL AND DONZ (*shock and pity*) No way!

*Enter Sam, Joe, Gabz, Jacky and Tone. Tone is bound in toilet paper now.*

DEZ Hey. Guess who here doesn't have a moby? 13

*All pupils bring out phones and flourish them – Tone rips through the toilet paper to do this.*

MRS PRESLEY Why am I not surprised at your disobedience, Milton Street?

| | |
|---|---|
| DEZ | But who's the odd man out? |
| MR YOUNG | Guilty. |
| MEL | Gutted. |

135

| | |
|---|---|
| NAT | How d'you survive, Sir? |
| JACKY | I'd die without mine. My finger jerks about mad-daft on its own if I haven't, like, texted anyone, like, for, like, five minutes. |
| DEZ | So how come you don't have a mobile, Sir? |

140

| | |
|---|---|
| MR YOUNG | Oh, they're marvellous things, I'm sure. But I just never felt the need, actually. |
| DONZ | How? No special phone-a-friends, Sir? |
| MEL | That's too sad. |
| NAT | We'd be your friends, Sir. |

145

| | |
|---|---|
| SAM | Speak for yourself. |
| JOE | De-cline. |
| MRS PRESLEY | (*losing patience*) Milton Street, I need a phone with a signal. Quick. So I can call this … Oh, I can't even make out the blasted name on this … (*peers at a leaflet*) |

150

| | |
|---|---|
| SAM | My phone's top spec. 3G Android. (*pause*) Aw, bummer. Signal's stuffed. |
| MRS PRESLEY | Anyone else? And it doesn't have to be the Ferrari of phones. Just one that works. |

155

| | |
|---|---|
| DONZ | Mine always works, Miss. |
| JOE | Nah. Look, dead as Jacky's love life. |
| JACKY | Ha! You think? |

**LEE** Mine's down too. My mum's really gonna flip it if she can't text me. 160

**MEL** Best keep that kind of info to yourself, Wheezy.

**LEE** Why? Just telling how it is. She'll flip. Not my fault.

**MRS PRESLEY** (*knocking on the closed door again*) Everyone, settle. I'm thinking. 165

**MR YOUNG** (*to Mrs Presley*) Hmmm, should we perhaps abandon ship, Morag? Have a stroll around the city centre? Take in the sights?

**MRS PRESLEY** Are you serious?

**MR YOUNG** Nip in for burgers and chips. My treat, of course. 170

**NAT** Someone say burgers and chips?

**MRS PRESLEY** (*aside*) Rupert, you're very kind, and I'm sure you mean well. But we are not taking these … these … anywhere serving food. (*whispers*) And please don't suggest it. It would not be a treat for you. Trust me on that. 175

**MR YOUNG** (*whispers*) We can't have the children standing here till our bus comes back, Morag.

**MRS PRESLEY** (*looks around at pupils, whispers*) We can't let them loose in public places, either. And forget burgers. Most of this group hold dining-hall life-bans for cutlery-throwing offences. As far as I'm concerned they're one evolutionary step away from chimpanzees. In the wrong direction. 180

**MR YOUNG** But it's cold and dark –

**MRS PRESLEY** I realise that, Rupert. Which is why I'm trying to think.

**SAM** So, Miss, we stuck here now till Bus the Bob comes back? 190

**DEZ** Are we?

**DONZ** Boo!

**JOE** I'd plans, Miss.

**JACKY** Was I part of them? 195

**JOE** Er, no.

**TONE** Don't wanna go back on the bus yet.

**LEE** Me neither.

**NAT** I'm thirsty again.

**MRS PRESLEY** Settle! And shush. We're going to try one last 200 time.

> *On Mrs Presley's signal, Mr Young knocks hard on the closed door.*

**SAM** Knock, knock, knock.

**JOE** Who goes there?

**SAM** Whoever you are don't get your hopes up. It's only Mr Young. 205

**MRS PRESLEY** Settle! If there's definitely no answer, we'll walk up to the main road and try to phone the bus company.

> *Mr Young knocks again. For the first time in the play, there is a long pause of silence.*

**MRS PRESLEY** I'm afraid we've had it, Milton Street.

**JACKY** Brilliant. 21

**MRS PRESLEY** Anyone need a last-minute visit to the toilet? Natalie?

**NAT** I'm all right.

**MRS PRESLEY** In that case –

**TONE** Wait! 21

**MRS PRESLEY** (*crossly*) For goodness' sake. Be quick!

**SAM** Slow Tone? Fat chance.

**TONE** I heard something.

**JACKY** Heard that, Sully!

**JOE** You'll smell it in a minute too. 22

**DONZ** Aw, I smell it already.

***Pupils all exclaim together.***

**\*LEE** Choking!

**\*SAM** (*laughing*) That's not funny, Joe!

**\*DEZ** Seen a doctor, man?

**\*TONE** Vet, more like! 22

**\*GABZ** Too right. You're a beast!

**\*JACKY** You're ill!

**\*NAT** You're toxic!

**TONE** Shhhh! Footsteps.

**MR YOUNG** I say! 23

**LEE** Someone's coming.

**GABZ** About time.

**DEZ** Is that a key?

**SAM** Here we go.

*The closed door now creaks open and there stands the Guide. She holds a lantern.*

**MRS PRESLEY** (*relieved*) So there *is* someone here.            235

**GUIDE** Good evening.

**GABZ** Er, not so far.

**MRS PRESLEY** The group from Milton Street School?

**SAM** Milton Street Massive!

**JOE** Yo-yo, whassup!            240

**MR YOUNG** For the Hidden City guided tour?

**GUIDE** Yes. I am the Guide.

**SAM** (*aside*) She's a big barrel of Cheesy Chuckles.

**MRS PRESLEY** We were just about to leave.

**GUIDE** That would have been unfortunate.            245

**MRS PRESLEY** We thought there was no one here.

**GUIDE** I am.

**MR YOUNG** We were knocking for quite some time.

**MRS PRESLEY** Didn't you hear us?

**GUIDE** I've come from a long way down. Shall we?            250

**MRS PRESLEY** Everyone!

**GUIDE** Follow me, please.

**MRS PRESLEY** Are you listening, Milton Street? Follow … Sorry, I didn't catch your name. I'm Morag Presley.

**GUIDE** It's going to be dark where we're going.            255

**MRS PRESLEY** Sorry, I still didn't catch your name …

*Blackout.*

# Scene Three

## Down the Hatch

*Everyone is gathered round an open hatch in the floor of the Hidden City Tours office. The only light comes from the Guide's lantern. The pupils jostle and fidget and banter.*

**\*SAM** (*nudging Lee towards hole*) Oops. You nearly fell in there.

**\*LEE** (*not impressed*) Ha. Ha.

**\*DONZ** Miss, Lee nearly fell in there.

**\*MRS PRESLEY** Settle! 5

**\*JOE** (*nudging Gabz, Jacky and Mel towards the opening*) You're gonna fall down too if you don't stop pushing like that.

**\*MEL** (*to Joe*) Quit it, twit!

**\*GABZ** (*to Joe*) You'll be down, head first. 10

**\*MR YOUNG** Now, now. That's a bit silly.

**\*JACKY** What? He's jostling *us*.

**\*MRS PRESLEY** Settle! No fighting!

**\*MR YOUNG** Quiet!

*Despite the reprimands from the teachers, overall authority seems to have shifted to the*

*Guide who faces the group, pausing the lantern on every character for a moment until a silence spreads and the fidgeting stops.*

**DEZ** So, Hidden City's down there, eh? 15

**SAM, GABZ, JOE AND JACKY** Wooooooooo …

**DONZ** Miss! It's a big black hole, Miss.

**MRS PRESLEY** I see that, Donna.

**LEE** Goes down and down and down and down and down and down and …/ 20

**MRS PRESLEY** /(*to the Guide*) This is safe, I take it?

**GUIDE** It's the way I take all my visitors down. (*to Lee*) Will you go first with the lantern?

**JOE** Soft Lee?

**SAM** Marshmallow McGee? No way. *I* should go first. 25

**LEE** I don't mind going first. Someone's got to.

**MR YOUNG** Well said there! That's the spirit!

**GUIDE** (*to Lee*) Ready?

**NAT** Ooooh. No way you'd get me down there on my own. 30

**MEL** Just black nothing.

**DEZ** Hey, and what if the ladder breaks? Or Lee faints like that time at the swimming pool?

**LEE** That was only cos Joe was dragging my legs down at the deep end and I stopped 35 breathing.

**SAM** 'Member, Miss, how you dived in with all your clothes on?

**JACKY** And your skirt flew up round your head and we totally saw your –                    4

**MRS PRESLEY** Thank you, Jacqueline.

**GABZ** Not exactly a pretty sight.

**LEE** (*to Joe*) And you got suspended for two weeks. And my dad went round to see yours.

**MRS PRESLEY** Settle!                    4

**GUIDE** (*to Lee*) Ready?

**MR YOUNG** Actually, perhaps I should go first. Safe pair of hands if anyone has a wobble on the ladder. Test the lie of the land.

**MRS PRESLEY** Good idea, Mr Young.                    5

**MR YOUNG** (*taking the lantern*) I'm a seasoned hillwalker, after all. Used to perilous descents in cruel weather, scree and snow and blinding blizzards –

**MRS PRESLEY** This is an inner-city tourist attraction, Mr Young. Not Everest.                    5

**LEE** Or that movie about the mad guy who sawed his own arm off.

**MR YOUNG** – so in the words of another intrepid hero: *I may be some time.*                    6

**DEZ** What movie?

**MRS PRESLEY** (*aside*) Just get on with it, Rupert.

*Mr Young descends.*

**MR YOUNG** Oh, I say, it's … Ooooh. Extremely dark. And this ladder's *raaa*ther unstable … Ugh!

| | | |
|---|---|---|
| **MRS PRESLEY** | Mr Young? (*pause*) Rupert? | **65** |
| **PUPILS** | *Rupert!* | |
| **MR YOUNG** | (*fainter*) It's quite all right, Morag. Just a bit … | |
| **MEL** | A bit what? | |
| **MR YOUNG** | *Eow!* | |
| **JACKY** | *Morag!* | **70** |
| **GABZ** | Totally looks like a Morag. | |
| **TONE** | That's cos she is one. | |
| **GABZ** | No, I mean her name's kinda like heavy-sounding and … like … Well, Morag rhymes with 'borag', yeah? | **75** |
| **TONE** | Is that a word? | |
| **LEE** | No. | |
| **GABZ** | And borag's like boring, innit? | |
| **JACKY** | Is it? | |
| **MRS PRESLEY** | Mr Young? | **80** |
| **MR YOUNG** | I'm fine. Oooh, ooooh, I say. There's a few strange … | |
| **DEZ** | Strange what? | |
| **MR YOUNG** | Just brushed up against – | |
| **JOE** | What? Hey, better flipping not be any big stringy – | **85** |
| **MR YOUNG** | Oh. Get off me! | |
| **NAT AND JOE** | Cobwebs? | |
| **MR YOUNG** | (*faintly*) Phew! Feet planted safe on dry land now. All present and correct. | **90** |

33

**DONZ** Sir? What's down there, Sir?

**MR YOUNG** Em … well. (*pause*) Nothing so far.

**GUIDE** (*to Lee*) Next?

**SAM** (*elbowing in front*) Laters. Wheeeeee!

*Sam practically flings himself down the hole.*

**MR YOUNG** (*from below*) Ow! 95

**GUIDE** Next?

**SAM** That your head getting in the way of my foot, Sir?

**JACKY** I'll go. Keep Sully company.

**GABZ** You're not leaving me up here. 10

*Gabz and Jacky jostle as they descend.*

**GABZ** Stop wobbling the ladder, Jacky.

**JACKY** Who's wobbling? I've not even put a foot on it yet. 'Ey, quit gawping up at me like that, Sam Sullivan.

**SAM** As if! 10

**JACKY** Gabz! Don't you dare back up! Want me falling to my death? I'm on my way … Eeek!

**JOE** What?

**JACKY** Something brushed right across my face.

**JOE** What did? 11

**JACKY** Cold thing.

**GUIDE** Next?

*Dez descends.*

**DEZ** What kind of thing? Did it feel like an icy finger?

34

**JOE** What kinda finger? 115

**LEE** Fish finger?

**TONE** Why'd there be fish fingers down a hatch? (*pause*) Hey, is there a café?

**NAT** Yeah!

**GUIDE** No. 120

**JOE** Better not be cobwebs.

**MEL** Better not be fingers.

**GUIDE** Next?

**DONZ** You going last, Miss?

**MRS PRESLEY** How can I leave any of you up here with an 125 open hatch?

**JOE** You don't think I'd shut it on you, Miss?

**MRS PRESLEY** Stranger things have happened around you before.

**TONE** D'you mean like when he locked you in the 130 book cupboard for April Fools?

**DEZ** And flushed the key?

**MRS PRESLEY** Quite.

**DONZ** Well, I'll go last with you, Miss.

**GUIDE** Next? 135

**MRS PRESLEY** Joe?

**JOE** Gonna wait with Donz.

**MEL** If you're waiting, I'm waiting.

**SAM** Hello? What's keeping everyone?

**GUIDE** Next? 140

**LEE** *Adios, amigos!*

*Lee descends, puffing and wheezing.*

**MRS PRESLEY** Take your time now, Lee. Don't panic.

**GABZ** Eeek, what the snortling?

**SAM** Wheezy McGee.

**LEE** That's me!                                               14

**JACKY** Should pay you to haunt this place. Just walk about breathing normally.

**LEE** Cheers. OK, that's me down.

**MR YOUNG** Well done, Lee! That was quick.

**GUIDE** Next?                                                   15

**NAT** Are there toilets down there?

**GUIDE** No toilets.

*Tone descends.*

**TONE** Ugh! Stinks.

**JOE** Whoever smelt it, dealt it.

**GUIDE** Next.                                                   15

**MRS PRESLEY** Go, Joe.

**JOE** Nat's ready.

**NAT** Can I just go quick to the toilet, Miss? I'm nervous, Miss.

**MRS PRESLEY** Nothing to be nervous about. You'll be back   16 up before you know it.

*Mrs Presley steers Nat on to the ladder.*

**MRS PRESLEY** Your turn next, Joe.

**JOE** Gad.

**NAT** (*mid-descent*) Ooooh, this is fun. Hey, and you
wanna see how scary movie your faces look all  165
tilted up round that light.

**GABZ** Can't be as scary as the sight of you clumping
down on top of us all.

**NAT** Ha ha.

**GUIDE** Next?  170

**MRS PRESLEY** Joe? Move.

**JOE** Mel?

**MEL** Nah, after you.

**GUIDE** Next?

**JOE** Nah, I'm cool.  175

**MEL** Frozen chicken, you mean.

*Joe takes a deep breath and descends quickly,
with several gasps and whimpers at first.*

**MEL** Fish fingers get you yet, Joe-Joe?

**JOE** Puh, just a ladder. Don't know why you're all
being wusses up there.

**MEL** Who's being a wuss?  180

*Mel descends.*

**GUIDE** Next?

**DONZ** Staying with you, Miss. Don't like heights, Miss.

**MRS PRESLEY** Well, we're not climbing down side by side.

**GUIDE** Who's next?

*Mrs Presley sighs and descends.*

**MRS PRESLEY** You just follow me, Donna. No, not as close as  185
that.

**DONZ** Oh, it's totally steep, Miss. And those laddery sticks you stand on –

**MRS PRESLEY** That would be rungs.

**DONZ** They're all mushy and squishy and moving. 19

**MRS PRESLEY** That's because your big hairy Uggs are on my shoulders, Donna.

**DONZ** Ooops.

**GUIDE** Everyone down?

**MRS PRESLEY** No, no. Not quite. 19

**SAM** (*in a deep voice*) Elvis is climbing into the building!

**MRS PRESLEY** I heard that, Sam Sullivan. Ow! Donna! That was my head!

**DONZ** Ooops. Sorry. Can't see a thing now. 20

**MRS PRESLEY** (*not quite at the bottom of the ladder*) Can you see if our guide –

**DONZ** She's just shutting the hatch over.

**EVERYONE ELSE** What?

**LEE** I think she's coming down now. 20

**MRS PRESLEY** (*to Guide*) Excuse me. Shouldn't the hatch be left open for –

> *Mrs Presley is interrupted by the sound of the hatch closing. The Guide descends.*

**SAM** I'd crack on, Miss. She's pretty nippy on her feet.

**LEE** She's flying , Miss!

**JOE** (*panicky*) So we're all closed in down here now? 21

**MEL** Scared, eh?

JOE As if. (*pause*) But why are we all closed in?

MRS PRESLEY Well, obviously there must be another exit if our guide's shutting – Oooof!

> *Mrs Presley and Donz reach the bottom*
> *followed immediately by the Guide, who*
> *retrieves the lantern from Mr Young.*

GUIDE All here? 215

MRS PRESLEY Gabrielle, Donna, Melanie, Jacqueline, Natalie, Lee, Sam, Desmond, Ant –

DEZ Are you counting Mr Young?

MR YOUNG Present, Mrs Presley.

DONZ Don't forget Tone, just cos he's quiet, Miss. 220

SAM Don't forget me, Miss. I'm quiet too.

MRS PRESLEY For goodness' sake, where was I? I can't seem to think.

TONE We're all here. Nine plus two teachers.

MRS PRESLEY We should have ten pupils! 225

MEL Tone, you count yourself?

> *Laughter, interrupted by:*

GUIDE So.

SAM So what?

GUIDE Welcome to what lies beneath your city.

SAM Woop-de-doo! 230

LEE Don't think we've actually started the tour actually.

MEL Tour of what, anyway?

JOE  We're just stood in a dark space.

GABZ  Brick walls.                                          23

SAM  Stone floor.

JACKY  Nothing.

MEL  Stinks.

JOE  Old.

NAT  Musty.                                                 24

MR YOUNG  It does, rather.

GUIDE  Three rules before we enter the first chamber.

DEZ  What chamber?

*The Guide moves off with the lantern.*

GUIDE  Rule one: follow me.

*The Guide swings round suddenly to check that rule one is being followed. The group, forced to stop, all bump into each other.*

*LEE  Hey!                                                  24

*NAT  Ow!

*MRS PRESLEY  Thank you, Donna, that was my big toe.

*DONZ  Sorry, Miss.

*MR YOUNG  I say, bit of a log-jam.

*TONE  Whassat?                                            25

*JOE  Pile up!

*SAM  Gabbo, are you an elephant?

*GABZ  Er, no.

*SAM  Someone's just broke my foot, stomping it.

*GABZ  Jacky!                                               25

**\*JACKY** Calling me an elephant, Missy?

**\*DEZ** Stop pushing!

**\*MRS PRESLEY** Settle!

**GUIDE** Good.

**MRS PRESLEY** Milton Street, are you listening? 260

**TONE** (*at the rear*) What?

**GUIDE** Rule two: everyone stay together.

**MRS PRESLEY** Sam Sullivan? No disappearing.

**DONZ** Like at the circus that time, Miss?

**JOE** When he stowed away in the clown's trunk? 265

**MRS PRESLEY** (*to Guide*) Made it on to a boat to Ireland, this one.

**GUIDE** Indeed? (*to Sam*) You like to wander off?

**SAM** Too right.

**GUIDE** Well, I should warn you; this place is a warren. 270

**JOE** Thought it was the Hidden City. Boom cha!

**GUIDE** (*to Sam*) You will never find your way out alone if you run away.

**MEL** That's comforting.

**SAM** Bet I would. 275

**GUIDE** (*to Sam*) No one has, believe me. (*pauses, addresses everyone*) Three: keep calm.

**MRS PRESLEY** Now, am I not forever telling you that, Milton Street? Calm down.

**GUIDE** I said: keep calm. 280

**MRS PRESLEY** Sorry?

TONE  What's the difference?

LEE  One means behave and the other's don't panic.

SAM  Cheers, Mastermind.  28!

JOE  Why'd anyone panic?

*Nat shrieks as Sam comes up behind her.*

MEL  What was that?

NAT  Sully, you better not pull that stunt again.

SAM  Can't stop me. I do what I like.

*The Guide starts walking with the lantern.*

JOE  Hey! I said why'd anyone panic?  29(

GUIDE  Follow me. Stay together. Keep calm. It's time to enter the first chamber.

*Blackout (literally, because the Guide turns a corner with the lantern).*

# Scene Four

## The Quiet Chamber

*By the light of the Guide's lantern, everyone huddles into a small, low ceilinged space with rubble floor and bare brick walls.*

**MRS PRESLEY** For goodness' sake, it's ridiculously dark in here.

**MR YOUNG** Terrifically dim, Morag. I hope it doesn't alarm any of the chil–

**MRS PRESLEY** *Thank* you, Mr Young. So where are the switches? 5

**GUIDE** There are no lights. But your eyes will get used to the dark once you've been in here a while. Mine have.

**MRS PRESLEY** But, surely, for Health and Safety in a public 10 attraction …?

**DONZ** Miss, I don't like this place much, Miss.

**MRS PRESLEY** I mean the floor surface is completely uneven. (*to Mr Young*) This is *not* what I was expecting from that leaflet you put on my – 15

**MR YOUNG** Leaflet, Morag?

**DONZ** Feels well spooky, Miss.

SAM (*to Donz*) 'Feels well spooky.' Boo-hoo. (*pause*) Does it heck. Feels nothing.

MRS PRESLEY (*to Mr Young*) The invitation leaflet. To come here. 20

*Mel, Donz, Lee and Tone are standing in a group, talking ion whispers.*

MEL (*whispers to Donz*) Hey, check out her face.

MR YOUNG I didn't give you any invitation leaflet, Morag.

DONZ (*whispers to Mel*) Who?

MRS PRESLEY No? 25

MR YOUNG No. You told *me* about the trip.

MEL Guide woman. You can't see her eyes any more.

MRS PRESLEY Are you sure, Rupert?

DEZ Whose eyes? 30

MEL Guide. Look. Her eyes have disappeared. Just seems like there's two empty holes –

LEE Sockets.

TONE Like for electric plugs?

MEL No. Sockets for eyes. Looks like there's big deep circles where hers should go. 35

NAT Man!

LEE Yeah, it's cos she's holding her lantern under her chin and it's throwing shadows on her face. Look round. There's shadows everywhere. 40

MEL Yikes. Did you have to say that?

**NAT** It's true. That one looks like a hunchback.

**MEL** Looming up behind the Guide.

**DONZ** Shurrup! 45

**MEL** But it does.

**LEE** Nah! It's just the shadow of the Guide stretched a bit.

**MEL** But the shadow doesn't match her shape.

**NAT** The arms are too long. 50

**LEE** The light's playing tricks, that's all.

**NAT** Wish it wouldn't.

**DEZ** D'you think a picture'll come out?

*Sam comes to the group.*

**SAM** Hey, better make sure you get me in.

*Dez takes a picture of the Guide with his phone. Sam poses beside her, pulling a cheeky, grinning face. The Guide appears not to notice. Before Dez can check his photo, Mrs Presley comes over to the group.*

**MRS PRESLEY** What's all the nonsense over here? 55

**DONZ** Miss, just saying I don't like these shadows.

**MRS PRESLEY** Settle, Donna, and stop muttering. And thank you, Desmond.

*Mrs Presley takes phone away from Dez.*

**MRS PRESLEY** (*to the Guide*) By the way, what am I expected to do if a pupil wanders off in the dark? 60

*Donz, Nat, Lee and Mel carry on whispering.*

**MEL** Her cheeks are all sunk in too.

**DONZ** Like a skull-head.

**LEE** Told you. Just shadows.

**NAT** It's like she's moving about. Changing shape.

**LEE** We look like *we're* moving and changing shape too. 65

**GUIDE** They were warned to stay together.

**MRS PRESLEY** You think this group heeds warnings?

**GUIDE** Unfortunate … (*pause*) Especially when these chambers are already full of unfortunate people. 70

> *The Guide gives one tiny, extremely short, high-pitched giggle. She immediately returns to her composed self.*

**MRS PRESLEY** (*frowning at the Guide*) Sorry?

**MR YOUNG** I think she said these chambers are already full of unfortunate people.

**MRS PRESLEY** (*whisper*) Thank you, Mr Young. I'm not deaf. 75 But what in the name of heaven does that even *mean*?

**GUIDE** Now. First things first.

> *The Guide produces some small torches.*

**SAM** (*aside to Joe*) Could have done with one going down that ladder. 80

**NAT** That's not enough.

**GUIDE** Share.

> *Sam and Joe share.*
>
> *Gabz and Jacky share.*

*Lee and Mel share.*

*Donz and Nat share.*

*Dez and Tone share.*

*The torches are weak and flickery.*

**SAM** Rubbish these, man. Can't see nothing.

**MRS PRESLEY** *Any*thing, you mean.

**SAM** I mean nothing. Can't see nothing. 85

**MRS PRESLEY** (*to Sam*) At least you've got one. (*to Guide*) Is there a torch for me and my colleague?

**GUIDE** No.

**DONZ** Miss, share with us, Miss. You share too, Sir.

**MR YOUNG** How kind! 90

**GUIDE** So. The first chamber.

*The Guide moves her lantern about slowly, and everyone tracks her with their torches. This first chamber seems to excite her, and she becomes quite girlish.*

**SAM** Wowee!

**GUIDE** Yes!

**SAM** Amazing.

**GUIDE** You're not the first of my visitors to say that. 95 Some are completely overwhelmed.

**MRS PRESLEY AND SAM** Overwhelmed?

**DEZ** Why?

**GUIDE** By its atmosphere. So very exciting.

**GABZ** Atmosphere? 100

**JOE** What's very exciting?

**JACKY** Hardly party central.

**GUIDE** (*giggles*) Some of my visitors actually have to leave. Immediately.

**JOE** Oh, I actually feel that. Deffo.          105

**GUIDE** You do?

**JOE** Yeah. Cos there's nothing to see, Miss. (*sings*) *Think I wanna leave right now.*

**MRS PRESLEY** Settle. No one's leaving.

**LEE** But why do some people leave?          110

**GUIDE** Because of how this chamber makes them feel.

**JACKY** Like bored –

**SAM** – out your box?

**GUIDE** Anxious. Unsettled. Nervy. Panicky sometimes.          115

**MR YOUNG** Well, it is rather claustrophobic. Very low ceiling. Thick sloping walls. Yes, you could understand some people might feel trapped and –

**DONZ** (*panicked by what Mr Young is saying*) Miss! Miss!          120

**MRS PRESLEY** *Thank* you, Mr Young.

**GUIDE** Others feel physically sick.

**TONE** That's me. Still. A bit.

**MRS PRESLEY** Oh, not now please, Anthony.

**GUIDE** Dizzy.          125

**MRS PRESLEY** Dizzy? I'm assuming there are no toxic fumes down here?

JOE Sort some out if you want. Toxic toots are my speciality.

*While Joe pulls fart faces, the following is said at the same time.*

*DONZ Miss! 130

*MRS PRESLEY Don't even think about it, Joseph.

*SAM Go on, my son! Let one go.

*MR YOUNG Must you? It's rather unpleasant.

*GABZ Don't bother.

*MEL Please don't bother. 135

MRS PRESLEY Settle! And I mean it. Don't you dare, Joseph.

GUIDE No fumes now. Although there were. Yes. Oh there definitely were. A long time ago. When these chambers were occupied.

MRS PRESLEY But it's safe? I need to know it's safe. 140

SAM (*creepily*) *Is it safe?*

GUIDE Well, I've spent a long time in these chambers and I'm perfectly comfortable down here. (*pause*) Although some of my visitors feel anything but safe. 145

MRS PRESLEY I beg your pardon?

MR YOUNG She said some visitors feel anything but –

MRS PRESLEY *Thank* you, Mr Young. I was actually wondering why any visitor might feel unsafe.

DEZ Is it maybe from coming down that wibbly- 150 wobbly ladder?

GUIDE No. Some of my visitors seem to experience a sense of overwhelming dread –

NAT, MEL AND JOE What?

DONZ Dread? 15

LEE That's a bad feeling.

TONE Thought it was a hairstyle.

SAM That's dreads, numbskull.

JOE Rasta man dreads, yeah.

GUIDE As if something unpleasant has happened 16 here.

NAT Yikes.

GUIDE (*smiles broadly*) Or could happen.

MEL (*aside to Nat*) Why she beaming her face off when she says that? 16

GUIDE (*to Sam*) So as you said when we came in: this chamber is *amazing*. Quite amazing. That so many of my visitors report different sensations in what's basically … (*pause*)

LEE An empty room? 17

GUIDE (*nods in agreement*) An empty room.

DONZ Miss, I don't like this empty room.

MEL Me neither.

GUIDE And so, welcome –

SAM (*horror-movie voice*) To the Chamber of 17 Nothing.

DONZ Stop it, you.

SAM (*horror-movie voice*) Walls and floor and er ...
That's all, folks.

JACKY Chamber of Nothing. Sam's spot on.                    180

GUIDE – to the start of your tour. Personally, I call this
the Quiet Chamber.

SAM (*horror-movie voice*) *Welcome to the Quiet
Chamber.* (*pause*) Why?

JOE Yeah, why's it called that?                             185

GUIDE Because there's relatively little activity in here.

TONE What she mean?

LEE By '*relatively*'?

MRS PRESLEY Ah. So there'll be activities further on?

GUIDE Without a doubt.                                      190

MRS PRESLEY Good. You had me worried. (*aside to the Guide*)
Because basically this *is* just an empty room.

GUIDE Or so it would seem.

MRS PRESLEY It *is* just an empty room. That's a fact.

GUIDE Well, you should tell that that to my visitors      195
who find things they can't explain on their
videos cameras after they've been here.

*The Guide flashes Mrs Presley a quick smile and
giggles again.*

*MRS PRESLEY Sorry?

*MEL Things they can't explain?

*MR YOUNG Oh, I say!                                        200

*DONZ Miss!

**\*SAM AND GABZ** Bah!

**\*LEE AND DEZ** What things?

**MRS PRESLEY** Oh, give me strength.

**SAM** Yeah, what things?     20

**GUIDE** Material that they can't explain.

**JOE** Material?

**JACKY** Like what? Velvet?

**GUIDE** Paranormal material.

**TONE** (*looking confused*) Para …?     21

**MR YOUNG** Oh, I say!

**GABZ** Is that not like …?

**LEE** Something that's not quite normal.

**DEZ** Like what?

**GUIDE** Oh, it varies. Bright moving lights that weren't   21
in the chamber when my visitors were –

**DEZ** Could just be camera flash?

**MRS PRESLEY** Of course it could.

**GUIDE** But more usually there are recorded images
of figures my visitors don't recall seeing when   22
they were in the chamber. Yes.

**DEZ** Figures?

**TONE** Like numbers?

**LEE** Like people, Tone.

**TONE** (*nodding but not understanding*) Ahh.   22

**MEL** People you don't see?

**GUIDE** Exactly. Standing by my visitors. Pointing at
them sometimes. Staring. Grabbing for them.

**DONZ** (*panicky*) Miss!

**GUIDE** Huddled in the corners. Appearing in what my 230
visitors swear was 'an empty room'.

> *As the group absorbs this information, the Guide*
> *swings her lantern over the chamber before*
> *moving to the exit.*

**GUIDE** I like to bring all my new visitors in here first.
As a test.

**TONE** Oh man, I hate tests.

**MRS PRESLEY** What kind of test?                                      235

**GUIDE** Some of my visitors don't cope beyond the
first chamber, you see.

**MRS PRESLEY** Cope?

**LEE** Cope how?

**GUIDE** If you're asking, you're ready to move on.    240
You've passed.

> *The Guide, almost mischieviously, pauses to take*
> *in the atmosphere of the chamber then exits.*

**GUIDE** Follow me.

> *Blackout.*

**TONE** I passed a test? I never pass tests.

# Scene Five

## The Cold Lady

*The group follows the Guide into a chamber identical to the first. The Guide's girlish mood is no more. She waits until everyone has settled before speaking.*

**GUIDE** So. A different chamber altogether. Yes?

**SAM** (*looking about*) She having a laugh?

*The Guide moves around the chamber with her lantern, the others track her with their torches.*

**NAT** Anyone freezing?

**LEE** Nah. Roasty-toasty.

**JOE** Mummy buttoned you into that stupid big bobbly fleece, that's why. 5

**LEE** I can dress myself, actually.

**GABZ** I wouldn't brag about it.

**MRS PRESLEY** Settle! And, everyone, spread out. Stop jostling. 10

**NAT** I can't stop shivering.

**GUIDE** So here we are. And I see one of you is already responding to this chamber.

**JACKY AND DEZ** We are?

**TONE** (*aside*) What's she mean?          15

**GUIDE** I'm not surprised.

**GABZ** About what?

**GUIDE** There's such a powerful presence in here.

> *The Guide looks around and gives another tiny,*
> *high-pitched giggle to herself. Only Mel notices.*

*****JOE** (*snort*) Yeah.

*****DEZ** Powerful what?          20

*****NAT** What presence?

*****JOE** Powerful boring.

**LEE** (*aside*) Hey, Mel. She kinda talking different to
you?

**MEL** Yeah. Maybe. Kinda. And did she just …?          25

**LEE** What?

**MEL** Nothing.

**NAT** Brr. The air's like ice.

**GUIDE** For over three hundred years this space has
stood, just as it is now.          30

**LEE** Wow!

**SAM** And why exactly are we here?

**JACKY** When there's nothing interesting going on.

**GUIDE** Exactly as it was when the Cold Lady perished.

> *A pause.*

**MRS PRESLEY** I beg your pardon?          35

**DONZ, NAT,
TONE, LEE,
DEZ AND MEL** The Cold Lady?

## Chamber of Nothing

**JACKY, GABZ**
**AND JOE** What Cold Lady?

**GUIDE** How tragic the final days of her life must have been.

**SAM** Woooohooooo. So it's the *haunted* chamber of nothing now? Bring it on! 40

**JOE** You serious?

**DONZ** Miss?

**SAM** Sh-sh-shaking an' a-quakin' is you, Joe?

**JOE** Gerroff. 45

**MRS PRESLEY** Settle.

**GUIDE** And no wonder her spirit lingers.

**MEL** No way.

**SAM** Having a laugh!

**JOE** Whose spirit? 50

**DONZ** The Cold Lady. Who is she?

**NAT** (*shivering*) And why's she called that? And why's this place so Ice Age?

**DONZ** Miss, Nat's totally shivering.

**SAM** (*mock shivering*) C-C-Cold Lady's c-c-coming to get to you. Whooooo … 55

**NAT** Stop it!

**GUIDE** It's no wonder certain visitors feel her chilly form swirling around them.

**DONZ** What? 60

**NAT** Certain visitors?

**MR YOUNG** Oh, I say.

**MRS PRESLEY** Natalie, you've caught a chill, that's all.
Running off to the toilet earlier was a sign. No
one else is cold.                                    65

**DONZ** Half of me's cold too, Miss. See the side near
Nat? Feels like there's a freezer door open or
something. Just here.

**NAT** That's what I've been feeling since I walked in.
From the top of my head and right down my     70
whole body.

**GUIDE** Now, whenever a cold sensation clings to one
of my visitors in this chamber –

**NAT AND DONZ** (*nervously*) Yeah?

**GUIDE** – it means the Cold Lady … (*pause*) She's here.   75

*Pupils exclaim in disbelief, anxiety and curiosity.*

*****SAM** Whooooo. (*pause*) No chance.

*****MR YOUNG** Oh, I say.

*****DONZ** Miss!

*****LEE** This place *is* meant to be haunted then?

*****DEZ** You think?                                      80

*****TONE** What?

*****GABZ** Cold Lady!

*****JACKY** Meet the Hot Lady!

*****JOE** Who's that then?

*****JACKY** Me, of course.                                85

*****NAT** Is that right?

57

MRS PRESLEY  Oh, for goodness' sake. Settle! (*to Mr Young*) Is this really the kind of information that leaflet mentioned?

MR YOUNG  I … I couldn't say, Morag. I told you I didn't read any –  90

MRS PRESLEY  Because I thought you said this sounded marvellous.

MR YOUNG  I meant an outing. Any outing. Anywhere. With the pupils. And it *is* marvellous. I'm thoroughly enjoying it.  95

MRS PRESLEY  You're easily pleased, Rupert.

LEE  (*to the Guide*) So who is she? This Cold Lady.

GUIDE  Well, she –

MRS PRESLEY  Lee, you should know better; there's no Cold Lady! Just a bit of a draught.  100

GUIDE  Ah, so you feel her too?

MRS PRESLEY  I certainly don't. (*mutters*) I don't feel anything except puzzled as to why we're huddled in another empty room hearing about things that don't exist.  105

GUIDE  (*stares at Mrs Presley*) Oh, Dorothea Blake exists. Her portrait hangs in the City Art Galleries.

GABZ, JACKY, SAM AND JOE  *Dorothea?*

MR YOUNG  Really?  110

GUIDE  She's the wife of Donald Blake, a wealthy tea merchant.

MR YOUNG  Fascinating.

**SAM** (*yawning*) Truly fascinating.

**MRS PRESLEY** Settle! 115

**GUIDE** Go back three hundred years ago: Dorothea is mistress of a very grand house. (*pause*) You are standing in its cellar.

**LEE** Ace!

**TONE** Doesn't look like *my* cellar. 120

**MEL** Hardly call this 'very grand'.

**MRS PRESLEY** (*aside to Mr Young*) Finally, some actual history. I must say, Rupert, this is definitely *not* what I expected.

**TONE** I keep my Wii down there. 125

**MRS PRESLEY** (*aside to Mr Young*) Thought at *least* there'd be a few, you know …? Feely boxes to keep this rabble entertained. Like in the museum. Interactive exhibits they can buzz and press and twiddle – 130

**GUIDE** In its day, Merchant Blake's house is one of the finest in this city. Its rooms – the many, many rooms above us – are brimming with furniture fashioned by master craftsmen the world over: tables of carved wood, dressers of 135 English oak, huge sturdy chests –

**JOE** (*sniggering*) Chests!

**SAM** (*sniggering*) Huge chests.

**MRS PRESLEY** Settle!

**GUIDE** Its drawing rooms and parlours and bedchambers are draped with embroidered silk, carpeted with thick rugs and hung with rich tapestries.

**SAM** Er, have I just been teleported to the Antiques Roadshow?

**GUIDE** Dorothea Blake herself is as stately as her home. In her portrait she is adorned in furs and amber and diamonds and pearls –

**SAM** Bling, bling, bro!

**GUIDE** – all marks of her mighty wealth, and symbols of her husband's devotion.

**JACKY** Lucky lady. I'm definitely finding me one of them minted blokes.

**MEL** Better start looking further than Milton Street now.

**GUIDE** Indeed, Dorothea Blake wants for nothing. That is, until Donald Blake returns from one of his trade expeditions bringing an exotic gift, not for Dorothea this time but for himself. She is young and very beautiful: the daughter of the Portuguese merchant in whose home he was a guest.

**SAM** Ooo-eee.

**GUIDE** And this young woman is carrying Donald Blake's child.

**TONE** All the way from Portugal?

**LEE** Not that kind of 'carry', mate.

**MEL** In-her-belly carry.

**MR YOUNG** Oh, I say.

**GABZ AND JACKY** Scandal! 170

**GUIDE** His first and only child, since Dorothea is barren.

**TONE** Huh?

**MRS PRESLEY** 'Barren' anyone? If a woman is barren it means –

**DONZ** Miss! Miss! 175

**MRS PRESLEY** Donna? Good girl!

**DONZ** I dunno what it means, Miss.

**MRS PRESLEY** Oh, for goodness' sake. 'Barren' means unable to bear children.

**TONE** Like a man, then. 180

**JOE** Or like you, Miss. You can't bear children.

**MRS PRESLEY** Nonsense.

**TONE** Always look well crabby when you see us.

**MRS PRESLEY** That's a different kind of 'bear' altogether, Tony. 185

**DONZ** So you *got* kids then, Miss? Wow! Can't imagine.

**JOE** (*aside*) Poor kids. The King for a ma.

**MRS PRESLEY** I heard that, thank you.

**NAT** Why am I so cold? 190

**GUIDE** (*quite loudly*) Ahem.

**MR YOUNG** So sorry. You were telling us about the merchant bringing home –

JOE His bit on the side.

SAM In the pudding club. 19

GABZ Up the duff.

JACKY Shock horror!

MRS PRESLEY I'm sure that kind of situation was quite common back then. I'm surprised this Donald chappy brought the girl home. She was only a 20 mistress, after all.

GUIDE Ah, but it's not so simple. Donald has fallen in love. He wants this young woman to be more than his mistress. Even more than that, he wants an heir. A legitimate heir. Dorothea is 20 replaced/

MEL /Totally happened to my Auntie Sharon, that. Uncle Darren, right, he comes swanning home with this new barmaid from down his local. Out the blue. Punts Auntie Sharon out. 21

MR YOUNG Dear, dear.

MEL S'all right. She found herself this hot new bloke on *meetyourmatch.com*. Ten years younger. Loadsa dosh.

MR YOUNG Oh, I say. 21

MEL Divorced Uncle Darren.

GUIDE But Donald can't divorce Dorothea. It would disgrace him. Ruin his reputation.

DEZ So did he chuck her out like Mel's auntie?

GUIDE Donald tries everything to make Dorothea 22 leave. He begs her. Offers her money. Property.

JACKY Take it and run, girl! I would.

SAM Golddigga!

GUIDE He promises to look after her for the rest
of her life. But Dorothea loves Donald. She    225
refuses to leave him.

SAM All right, so he just do her in to get rid?

GUIDE Well.

*A pause.*

DONZ What?    230

SAM He done her in, didn't he? Bet ya!

JOE Killah!

GUIDE Actually, he banishes her.

TONE Is that like bashes?

GABZ Brainshare.    235

DEZ Thought she wouldn't leave?

GUIDE That's why he banishes her to this cellar.
(*pause*) He locks her away.

NAT Where we're standing?

DONZ Miss!    240

DEZ How'd he get away with that?

GUIDE He tells everyone that his beloved Dorothea
will be at his side on his next long voyage. The
house is closed up, the servants dismissed
and Merchant Blake's ship sets sail for the    245
other side of the world.

LEE And everyone thinks –

GUIDE – Dorothea is on board. But no.

**MR YOUNG** She's walled up in this cellar.

**GUIDE** No food. No water. 25

**JOE** So she rots away?

**NAT** In this room?

**GUIDE** In this room.

**LEE** For real?

**MRS PRESLEY** How on earth did the husband get away with 25
that?

**LEE** He moved abroad, started a new life, right?

**DEZ** Like a gangsta on the run?

**GUIDE** Donald Blake remains abroad for over two
years. When he does return – with a new wife 26
and his baby son – he regales the tragedy of
his first wife, Dorothea, to anyone who will
listen. How she fell overboard in a storm. How
her body is lost at sea.

**SAM** Fish food, man. 26

**NAT** Only she dies in here?

**GUIDE** Of hunger. Of thirst. And, of course, of cold.

**MR YOUNG** Quite fascinating.

**MRS PRESLEY** But how exactly do you know this?

**SAM** Yeah, how? 27

*A pause.*

**GUIDE** I know because I'm the Guide of these
chambers. (*pause*) And because the Cold Lady
still makes her presence felt. (*suddenly pointing
at Nat*) She's there.

*Pupils and teachers all peer at Nat. While they
do this the Guide gives another tiny giggle.
Again, only Mel notices.*

GABZ Don't see nothing. 275

MRS PRESLEY *Any*thing.

GABZ Whateva.

GUIDE You're there, aren't you, Dorothea? I hope
we're not disturbing you too much.

JOE Did she just talk to someone who's not there? 280

SAM She's having a laugh!

JOE Creeping me out whatever she is, man.

MEL Me too.

GUIDE So, shall we move on?

JOE AND NAT (*quickly*) Yeah. 285

MRS PRESLEY And what about these activities you
promised? Are there some in the next room?

GUIDE I guarantee it. Follow me.

*The Guide leaves the chamber followed by Mrs
Presley and the others. Donz, Nat and Mr Young
bring up the rear.*

DONZ Miss, wait! I'm with you, Miss.

MR YOUNG Bearing up, Natalie? That was fascinating. 290

NAT (*shivering*) Nah, freezing. Think it's really the
Cold Lady?

MR YOUNG Oh, now, we're deep in the bowels here.
I'm sure it's just normal chill –

NAT But feel my shoulder. 295

> *Mr Young reaches to touch Nat, but recoils before he makes contact.*

**MR YOUNG** By Jove!

**NAT** Told you.

> *Leaving the chamber, Nat looks at her shoulders with the torch, shrugging as if she feels something. The torch appears to swipe from her hand and go out with a clatter and a smash. Nat screams.*

**MR YOUNG** Oh I say!

**DONZ** Miss!

> *Blackout.*

# Scene Six

## The Cobbler's Chamber

*The third chamber. Again, it is basically identical*
*to the first and second, although, for variety, the*
*group might 'enter' from a different angle.*

**DONZ** … that's me and Nat with no light now, Miss.

**MRS PRESLEY** Oh, for pity's sake. You can't be trusted if I turn
my back two sec–

**NAT** But the torch just flew right out my hand!

**SAM** Flew? Puh! 5

**MRS PRESLEY** So you dropped it.

**NAT** No. It just flew. Like it was whacked or
something. It whooshed out my hand.

**MRS PRESLEY** By a draught, in other words.

**MR YOUNG** Oh, something stronger. A whipping gust of 10
icy … Like someone close, sweeping past –

**MRS PRESLEY** *Thank you*, Mr Young.

**NAT** See? Not just me who felt what I felt, Miss.

**DONZ** That Cold Lady woman, Miss. Musta been her.

**MRS PRESLEY** Don't be ridiculous! 15

**NAT** Miss. See back there. I was sure I felt a
presence –

**MRS PRESLEY**  Listen. I'm having no hysterics. Carelessness – that's what made you drop your torch. In fact, go back and fetch it, Natalie. I can barely see   20 my hand in front of me as it is.

**NAT**  Miss, I can't go back along there myself. It's miles!

**DONZ**  She can't, Miss. And the Cold Lady's in there anyway, Miss.   25

**SAM**  *Whooooooo!*

**NAT**  Don't even want to stay down here. Can I not just go back up? Wait in the office?

**MRS PRESLEY**  You're staying here. We're all staying. Now fetch that torch.   30

**NAT**  But the Cold Lady, Miss.

**MRS PRESLEY**  There is no Cold Lady.

**NAT**  Why was I totally frosty then?

**DONZ**  She was, Miss.

**MRS PRESLEY**  She wasn't. It's a story.   35

**DONZ**  She was, Miss.

**MR YOUNG**  And I must say, I definitely felt … well almost a … a *halo* of icy –

**MRS PRESLEY**  *Thank you*, Mr Young –

> *The Guide keeps her voice quite raised in this section, as if speaking above background noise.*

**GUIDE**  So, if I might begin. We've reached the third   40 chamber of our tour./

**NAT**  /Can I not go back up please, Miss?

**MRS PRESLEY** You can go and find that torch.

**NAT** No way!

**MRS PRESLEY** Calm down! 45

**NAT** Can one of the boys not go?

**DEZ** Are you joking?

**SAM** Go yourself, scaredy puss.

**JOE** Thought it was smashed anyway.

**LEE** *I'll* go. 50

**TONE** It's pretty far.

**DEZ** Weren't we to stay together?

**GUIDE** Yes. No one should ever wander alone down here. And there's no point looking for a broken torch. So, if I might continue, this 55 chamber –

**DEZ** Ow! Who punched me?

**TONE** Don't think I did.

**DEZ** Whoever it was, you gonna quit?

**MEL** And see whoever's tapping, you gonna quit 60 that too?

**GUIDE** (*louder*) *This* chamber –

**LEE** What about this chamber?

**MRS PRESLEY** (*to Mel*) What tapping?

**SAM** You're hearing things, girl. 65

**JOE** Unless it's Nat's teeth.

**NAT** I've stopped shivering FYI.

GUIDE (*over the chat*) – would have been full of
activity –

DEZ (*to Nat*) How come? 70

NAT I just stopped. Not cold any more.

LEE Wow!

MEL Can nobody hear that: *tap-tap-tap*? (*pointing
to a corner of the chamber*) It's coming from
there. 75

GUIDE (*over the chat*) – because it used to be –

GABZ AND
JACKY Where?

TONE What's from there?

MEL Flaming non-stop *tapping*! You got cloth ears?

SAM As well as a cloth brain? 80

LEE Can't hear tapping. Anyone else?

TONE, NAT
AND DONZ Nah.

GUIDE (*over the chat*) – it used to be –

MEL You're all cloth ears then.

*SAM What? 85

*JOE Somebody speak?

*GABZ I didn't hear no one.

*MRS PRESLEY *Any*one.

*JACKY Didn't hear no one neither.

MR YOUNG (*moving to check where Mel had been pointing to* 90
*and stumbling over his feet, nearly falling*) I say.

*Sam, Joe, Gabz and Jacky snort and guffaw.*

SAM Enjoy your trip, Sir?

MR YOUNG  No one over there, Melanie.

MRS PRESLEY  Of course there isn't. So settle!

GUIDE  (*louder*) So *this* chamber, according to records, 95
used to be/

MEL  /That sound's drilling into my skull.

GUIDE  /(*even louder*) a cobbler's workshop.

LEE  Wow.

SAM  Cobblers? Still is. 100

JACKY  Cobblers. Lol.

GUIDE  John Mair is the cobbler.

MR YOUNG  Marvellous to have an actual name. Always
makes a place feel more alive.

GUIDE  Yes. 105

LEE  Yeah.

SAM  (*sarcastic*) Yeah?

MEL  *Brrr*. A huge giant shiver just ran right down
my back, there.

SAM  The Cold Lady's cold fingers are freezing *your* 110
bones now, baby. *Whooooooo*.

JOE  Shurrup.

JACKY  What you calling her 'baby' for? She's a big
grown-up girl.

SAM  You think? 115

GUIDE  Can you picture his workplace I wonder?

SAM  Er. Let me see ... (*pause*) No. All I picture's
another stupid old bare brick nothing-
happening-on-it wall.

**GUIDE**  Well, let's see if I can help with that. I don't   1:
know whether anyone noticed that the
passage we've just walked brought us slightly
uphill –

**LEE**  My lungs noticed.

**GUIDE**  – which tells us this room must have been   1:
near street level at one time.

**MR YOUNG**  How fascinating.

**SAM AND JOE**  (*yawning*) *Fascinating!*

**MRS PRESLEY**  Settle!

**GUIDE**  And it would have had the same bare walls   13
you see now. Thick.

**SAM**  Thick like Tone.

**MRS PRESLEY**  Settle!

**GUIDE**  And it would have been very damp indeed.

**GABZ**  Gross!   13

**MR YOUNG**  Fascinating!

**SAM**  (*aside*) He's gotta be having a laugh.

**GUIDE**  With the same faint light, despite its window.

**TONE AND
MRS PRESLEY**  Window?

**GUIDE**  Over there. See? The outline in the stone?   14

**DONZ**  Miss, I see it. Different colour brick, Miss.

**MEL**  And me.

**LEE**  Yeah.

**MRS PRESLEY**  Good. Can't say I do.

**JACKY**  Me neither. Don't see nothing.   14

**MRS PRESLEY** *Any*thing.

**MEL** (*hands over ears*) Is no one else hearing that?

**GUIDE** Of course, there was no glass in the window. It's basically a hole for light and ventilation. Not very good ventilation either. This chamber 150 is a miserable place for John Mair to work –

**JOE** (*mutters*) Not as miserable as it is to visit.

**SAM** Five thousand years later.

**JACKY** Lol.

**GUIDE** – with the winds howling and rain lashing in, 155 churning the earthen floor to mud.

**JOE** Cobbler bloke shoulda borrowed a fancy rug from that Cold Lady.

**GUIDE** Then, of course, in the summer heat, it swelters in here. It grows stale. Airless. 160 Unhealthy. Foul.

**JOE** Sounds like my bedroom.

**GUIDE** The perfect breeding ground for the fatal disease –

**GABZ** Definitely sounds like your bedroom. 165

**MR YOUNG** Fatal disease?

**GUIDE** – that strikes John Mair as he labours at his last.

**SAM** His last what?

**LEE** Cobblers fixed shoes on a last. 170

**GABZ** Wait. And you know stuff like that how?

**SAM** Yeah, Mastermind?

| | |
|---|---|
| **LEE** | Dunno. |
| **GABZ** | Not him. (*to Guide*) *You* know stuff like that how? |

| | |
|---|---|
| **GUIDE** | Good question – |
| **MRS PRESLEY** | (*interrupting*) Now that *is* actually a good question, Gabrielle. |
| **JACKY** | Ooooh, Presley's pet. |
| **GABZ** | Shurrup. |

| | |
|---|---|
| **JACKY** | Ow, Gabzers! No need to pinch. Just kidding. |
| **GABZ** | I didn't pinch! |
| **JACKY** | Ow! Done it again. |
| **GABZ** | *Didn't*. Nutter. |
| **MRS PRESLEY** | Settle! |

| | |
|---|---|
| **JACKY** | Ow! Cow. |
| **GUIDE** | The reason *I* know so much about John Mair – |
| **MRS PRESLEY** | If I could perhaps interrupt for two … So, Milton Street. How *would* someone like … (*to Guide*) Sorry, I still haven't caught your – |

> **The Guide looks at Mrs Presley but remains silent.
> Mrs Presley turns her attention back to the pupils.**

| | |
|---|---|
| **MRS PRESLEY** | How would we go about tracing the history of a place like this? And the people in it? |
| **MR YOUNG** | *Ahem*, our guide did mention records, Mrs Presley. |
| **SAM** | Like 'Blue Suede Shoes'! That's one of your records, Miss. And (*sings in Elvis mumble*) *a little more understanding, a little more –* |

| | |
|---|---|
| **MRS PRESLEY** | Thank you, Sam, and *thank you*, Mr Young. Apart from that? |
| **DONZ** | Miss! 200 |
| **MRS PRESLEY** | Anyone? |
| **LEE** | Old stuff gets dug up. Like on *Time Team*, Miss. |
| **MR YOUNG** | Marvellous programme! |
| **DEZ** | With those beardy men in the mad jumpers? |
| **MRS PRESLEY** | Like on *Time Team*, yes! Producing artefacts 205 we can date. |
| **JOE** | Arty farts? |
| **SAM** | Date like take to the pictures, Miss? |
| **MRS PRESLEY** | No. |
| **SAM** | Hey, broken old pot. Fancy *Toy Story 3* and a 210 jumbo bucket of popcorn? |
| **JACKY** | Date, ha! Ow! (*smacks Gabz*) Cow. |
| **GABZ** | Whassat for? Didn't touch you. |
| **DONZ** | Or maybe our guide found dead bodies, Miss? |
| **MEL** | No way. 215 |
| **DONZ** | Buried down here with their clothes and teeth and bones and that? |
| **JOE** | Stiff stiffs. |
| **DONZ** | Bet there *are* dead bodies down here, Miss. Loads, Miss. Feels it to me, Miss. 220 |
| **SAM** | Like the Cold Lady. *Whooooo.* |
| **MEL** | Quit it. |
| **SAM** | How? |

| MEL | Cos this place feels creepy enough without you going all Freddy Krueger. | 22 |

TONE Who?

MEL That tapping's horrible.

GUIDE I'm delighted to see another of my visitors responding to the presences down here.

JOE, NAT AND TONE Huh? 23

LEE Why's she's looking at you, Mel?

MRS PRESLEY For goodness' sake, no one's responding to anything. They're just all winding each other up, because that's what they do better than spelling and reading and – 23

GUIDE (*to Gabz*) Oh, and if I might answer *your* question.

GABZ My question?

JACKY Suck up.

GABZ Shurrup. Ow! Did you pinch *me* now? 24

JACKY Nup.

MRS PRESLEY Settle!

GUIDE About my knowing who occupied this chamber? Apart from the records, we have first-hand evidence a cobbler worked over in that corner – 24

MEL Where the tapping's coming from?

GUIDE Yes. (*pause*) That's how we know.

*MEL Come again?

*DEZ Did she just say the tapping's how we – 25

*LEE – know about some guy?

*NAT Dead guy.

*DONZ Miss!

*SAM Whassis?

*MR YOUNG Oh, I say! 255

GUIDE (*to Mel*) Can be disturbing, can't it? John Mair's tap-tap-tapping.

*The Guide give another smothered giggle.*

MEL What?

GUIDE It's a hollow sound. Slightly muffled.

MR YOUNG Oh, I say. 260

GUIDE As if his hammer is wrapped in cloth, perhaps.

MRS PRESLEY Nonsense.

JACKY Er, if a dead cobbler's tapping, does that not mean this place is kinda haunted?

SAM (*making ghost noises*) *Whooooooo!* 265

JACKY (*to Sam*) No need to poke me, you. Just saying does that not mean this place is haunted?

SAM What? I didn't lay a finger on you.

GABZ (*to Jacky*) Ow! Poke *him* back, not me!

JOE Girrrrl fight. 270

MRS PRESLEY Settle!

GUIDE Of course this place is haunted. All the chambers are.

*DEZ Come again?

*SAM Having a laugh? 275

**\*DONZ** Miss, did she say *haunted*? All of it. She said it's all –

**\*MR YOUNG** Oh, I say!

**\*MRS PRESLEY** Settle! Nothing's haunted.

**\*TONE** So how come she just said …?

**\*SAM** *Whooooooo!*

**\*GABZ** You mind not pinching while you blow down my ear.

**\*SAM** Huh? Pinch? Not guilty.

**\*JACKY** (*to Joe*) Or pulling hair. Got my GHDs to straighten it, thanks.

**\*JOE** Didn't touch your skanky hair.

**GUIDE** And it's no wonder. (*pause*) Now, apart from the tapping you hear, some visitors also *see* John Mair's silhouette.

**TONE** Huh?

**LEE** That means his outline.

**DEZ** Eh, what d'you mean by 'no wonder'?

**GUIDE** He's tall and very thin. Hunched over. Perhaps one of you can … ?

*The Guide holds her lantern over to the corner.*

**DONZ** Miss!

**LEE** (*to the Guide*) Have *you* seen him?

**GUIDE** Of course. I hear him too. Coughing. Don't I, John?

**DONZ** (*panicking*) Miss!

**NAT** I really can't stay down here any longer.

**MRS PRESLEY** (*to the Guide*) Ahem, I'd no idea this was the
kind of information you were going to … It's
not really suitable for these –

**GUIDE** His arm hammers up and down and up and      305
down and up and down.

**DEZ** (*to the Guide*) What did you mean by 'no
wonder' a minute ago?

**MEL** Miss, think that's the tapping? This cobbler
man?      310

**SAM** Dead cobbler man.

**MRS PRESLEY** No! And there's no tapping.

**MEL** Because, see, if there is …

**LEE** The ghost of a cobbler. Right here. Wow!

**MR YOUNG** Fascinating!      315

**MRS PRESLEY** Really!

**SAM** (*sarcastic*) Yeah. Pile of poo, more like.

**MRS PRESLEY** Language!

**JOE** Better be a pile of poo, or I'm outta here too.

**SAM** (*making chicken noises*) Buck, buck, buck.      320

**JACKY** I'm with you, Joe-Joe.

**GABZ** Thought you were with Sam? Make your mind
up. (*pause*) Ow!

**JACKY** What?

**GABZ** What'd you claw my neck for? I was just      325
ribbing, Jacks.

**JACKY** Who?

GUIDE  Aha. Now, as some of you are finding out, John Mair doesn't live in here alone.

LEE  *Live?*  33

DEZ  How d'you mean 'finding out'?

JACKY  Ow! (*to Gabz*) Dug your nails into my hand there too.

GABZ  Did I heck!

DEZ  (*to Mrs Presley*) Miss, d'you not think she should say what she meant by 'no wonder'?  33

JACKY  Miss, Gabz keeps scratching me.

GABZ  She's scratching *me*.

MRS PRESLEY  Settle. Scratching counts as fighting, remember.  34

TONE  But not if you're itchy?

GUIDE  We know John Mair shares this chamber with his wife. And seven children.

SAM  No way. Seven squashed kids in here?

DEZ  This tidgy dump?  34

LEE  Lives? Shares? (*to Tone*) D'you not notice she keeps talking in the present tense.

TONE  The what?

LEE  Like that cobbler and his kids are here. *Now.*

GABZ AND JACKY  Ow!  35

GUIDE  Meg, Alice, Jane, Kate, Mary, Anne. All registered in the city's records of birth –

MEL  That tapping's getting faster and harder.

MRS PRESLEY It'll be an old pipe rattling.

DONZ All girls.                                            355

GUIDE – and records of death. And there's one son. He dies stillborn. Unnamed. With Grace Mair, his mother …

MR YOUNG Dear, dear. A sad place then.

GUIDE Dreadfully.                                          360

JOE Tell me they don't die in here.

GUIDE Oh, they all die in here. I told you.

SAM (*to Joe*) Keep up.

GUIDE Fatal disease claims their lives. One by one.

JACKY What?                                                365

GUIDE Probably typhus, although it's not identified as such in the records.

MR YOUNG Oh, I say.

*LEE Fatal disease.

*SAM Awesome.                                              370

*GABZ *Awesome?* Are you totally sick, Sully?

*JOE (*sniggering*) Hope not.

*DEZ Was it infectious?

*JACKY Duh. What d'you think? Clue: 'fatal'.

*GABZ Disease.                                             375

*MEL Yikes.

*DONZ Miss!

MRS PRESLEY Settle!

GUIDE Now, in better times this chamber is a hive
of activity. (*she points at various places in the* 38
*chamber*) John Mair's work bench and his tools
are there. The fireplace with its cooking pot
and utensils hanging there.

DEZ How d'you know that?

GUIDE I'm the Guide. I know everything about these 38
chambers. (*pause*) And there's charring on the
bricks here. Grease stains.

LEE Oh yeah.

MR YOUNG The remains of a hearth perhaps.

GUIDE Exactly. A sleeping area here. Close to the 39
heat. Just sacks and straw, of course.

SAM (*sarcastic*) Of course.

GUIDE And in the middle of the room the girls old
enough to work sit cross-legged.

DEZ Where? 39

GUIDE (*to Mr Young*) Where you tripped.

MR YOUNG Oh, I say!

GUIDE Someone always trips. I should really warn –

MR YOUNG I *thought* I felt something soft –

MRS PRESLEY Mr Young, really! 40

LEE Really?

JOE This is starting to be not funny.

NAT I'm going to have to get out.

DONZ Miss, Nat's breathing all fast and squeaky.

JOE Her and Lee could do a duet. 40

LEE Ha ha. Hilarious. Not.

DEZ How can you know where these dead kids worked?

GUIDE Apart from my visitors tripping over them?

NAT Stop it! 410

MRS PRESLEY Natalie, stay beside me. You're fine.

MEL Miss, do we have to stay in here much longer?

GABZ Ow!

JOE Do we?

GUIDE I find dropped needles sometimes. 415

SAM Like junky needles?

GUIDE (*to Sam*) No. (*looks around the chamber and smiles*) And of course I see them.

*The Guide gives another sudden, manic, high-pitched giggle.*

JOE What was that all about? 420

TONE What?

JACKY Freak out!

DONZ Miss!

MEL *Do* we have to stay in here much longer?

GUIDE (*slightly sing- song*) Kate, Mary, Anne – they can be quite the little minxes. Pinching, poking, 425 punching, playing tricks.

GABZ Blowing? Like this? *Whhhhhh.* In your face?

GUIDE Tugging hair. Flitting in and out. Scratching with their sharp little nails.

JACKY Ow! 430

GUIDE (*her voice deepens*) Naughty minxes, aren't you?

DEZ Whoa. Who's she talking to now?

JOE In a man's voice. And stop grabbing at me with your scaly mitts, Jacko. 435

JACKY I didn't! And my hands are lovely BTW.

GUIDE Can't blame them for having fun.

JOE (*to Jacky*) Who did then?

GUIDE However, they weren't exactly frolicking when the chamber was discovered. 440

DEZ (*mutter*) Do I want to hear this?

GUIDE (*to Dez*) Well, you asked why I said 'no wonder'? You shouldn't ask questions unless you want the answers.

MRS PRESLEY Listen, I'm never done telling this pest – 445

GUIDE So when one by one the family falls ill – and that happens very quickly indeed – they're quarantined in this chamber. At first, neighbours help them. Passing water and food through the window. But as people 450 realise how sick the family is becoming – riddled with disease, raving with fever – the window is sealed.

MR YOUNG How dreadful.

GUIDE People are terrified, you see, of infection spreading. 455

LEE So the family's left to die?

| | |
|---|---|
| **GUIDE** | First the mother with her stillborn son. Then the little girls. |
| **MR YOUNG** | Oh, I say. |
| **GUIDE** | Moaning, sighing, weeping with sores – |
| **MRS PRESLEY** | I think we get the picture. |
| **MEL** | Miss, there's a really bad vibe down here. |
| **MRS PRESLEY** | (*to Mel*) Shhh. Listen. |
| **GUIDE** | John Mair, fever-crazed himself, is tortured by the agony of his daughters. Sobbing for their mother as their lives ebb away … |
| **MR YOUNG** | Dear, dear./ |
| **MEL** | /That hammering won't stop! |
| **GUIDE** | So who can blame him using the last of his strength to put his children out of their misery? |
| **TONE** | Huh? |
| **GUIDE** | Taking up his hammer. (*pause*) Tapping the lives from his daughters one by one. |
| **SAM** | What? Saying he bashes their brains out? |
| **DEZ** | His own kids? |
| **JOE** | With a hammer? |
| **TONE** | Sick! |
| **MEL** | Horrible! |
| **SAM** | Musta been blood totally everywhere. |
| **NAT** | Don't! |
| **GUIDE** | I suppose some would call it mercy killing. |

460

465

470

475

480

| | |
|---|---|
| **MRS PRESLEY** | I'd call it mass murder. And I don't believe a word. |
| **MR YOUNG** | Oh, I say. |
| **MEL** | Don't say that's what I'm hearing. Please don't say that's what I've been hearing! |
| **MRS PRESLEY** | Of course it's not, Melanie. It's pipes. (*half-addressing the Guide*) How could it possibly be? |
| **GUIDE** | How could it possibly be indeed? In an empty room. Nothing to show for nine lives but the outline of a window and a few charred bricks. (*walks to the exit of the chamber*) Shall we move on? Follow me. |

> *Exit the Guide followed obediently by Lee. The others hang back.*

| | |
|---|---|
| **MEL** | Miss? |
| **DONZ** | Miss. Mel's breathing all funny now too. |
| **MR YOUNG** | Hyperventilating. |
| **MRS PRESLEY** | Thank you, Mr Young. I see that. |
| **MEL** | Miss, I'm done. |
| **NAT** | This is a horrible place. |
| **MEL** | I don't want to hear that tapping any more. What if it's that man, hammering his own little – |
| **JACKY, JOE AND GABZ** | Shurrup. |
| **SAM** | Total bloodbath it musta been. Eighteen-plus horror movie. Can you see it? |
| **MEL** | Stop it, sicko. |
| **MRS PRESLEY** | Look, there's no tapping. |

**MEL** But I can still hear it, Miss.

**MRS PRESLEY** It's your imagination. 510

**DEZ** Thought you said pipes?

**MRS PRESLEY** Or pipes.

**NAT** What about me shivering? I was frozed, Miss.

**MRS PRESLEY** Frozen.

**NAT** Ask Mr Young. 515

**MR YOUNG** Actually there *was* a definite layer of icy –

**MRS PRESLEY** *Thank you*, Mr Young. The cold was your imagination too, Natalie.

**JACKY** Thought you said she'd got a chill. (*mutters*)
Make your mind up, Elvis. 520

**MRS PRESLEY** I heard that, Jacqueline.

**DEZ** Miss, so we not going into the next room now?

**TONE** That guide woman said 'follow me'.

**JOE** Freak out! You can hear her speaking and she's 525
not even in here.

**TONE** No. That was her rule: follow me.

**NAT** I don't want to follow her any more, Miss.

**DONZ** Stuff her rules.

**MEL** She's creepy. And what if there's more 530
tapping? What if there's worse?

**MRS PRESLEY** How can there be worse than nothing? Look
around. There's nothing. This place is a con.

**SAM** Why are we here then?

| | |
|---|---|
| **MRS PRESLEY** | Well! For once in our lives we're singing from the same hymn-sheet, Sam Sullivan. |

535

| | |
|---|---|
| **DONZ** | I don't hear you hymn singing. Do you hear singing? |

| | |
|---|---|
| **DEZ AND TONE** | Singing? |

| | |
|---|---|
| **DONZ** | Hymns. |

540

| | |
|---|---|
| **MRS PRESLEY** | No one's singing hymns! |

| | |
|---|---|
| **MEL** | Phew! |

| | |
|---|---|
| **TONE** | But you said you and Sam – |

| | |
|---|---|
| **MRS PRESLEY** | Oh, give me strength. I was using a figure of speech. Remember we looked at them in English last week when we read the poem about the tiger? |

545

| | |
|---|---|
| **TONE** | Did we read a poem? |

| | |
|---|---|
| **DONZ** | Ah, Miss, is figure of speech when you speak in that like shaky weird voice just before you lose your – |

550

| | |
|---|---|
| **MRS PRESLEY** | (*losing her rag and speaking in a shaky weird voice*) No! It means I was agreeing with Sam when he asked why are we here. |

| | |
|---|---|
| **MR YOUNG** | I say, that is the big question: why is anybody here? The meaning of life. |

555

| | |
|---|---|
| **MRS PRESLEY** | Mr Young, why would I suddenly be looking for the meaning of life? |

| | |
|---|---|
| **GABZ** | (*to Sam*) With Sully. In the dark. |

*Mrs Presley herds the group from the chamber.*

MRS PRESLEY  (*aside to Mr Young*) Honest to goodness, Rupert.  560
The sooner we see the next godforsaken
'chamber' (*pause*) Of nothing … Huh! You
know for once that clown Sam Sullivan's right.
There is nothing but chambers of nothing
in here. We'll be done and dusted and out,  565
and I'll be writing one of my letters to the
management of this caper. Because it cannot
*possibly* be the same tour my brochure –

*A high-pitched female shriek.*

DONZ  *Miss!*

*Blackout.*

# Scene Seven

## The Prison Chamber

*The group are crowded at the entrance to the fourth chamber, which again looks like the ones before. Lee and the Guide are waiting inside. Gabz is angry and shaken.*

**GABZ** Think you're bigstyle ha-ha-ha?

**SAM** That *was* bigstyle ha-ha-ha. *I* thought so.

**JOE** Some set of foghorn bellows on you, Gabbo. Half-deafened me. Just messing!

**GABZ** You'd be messing your pants if two dipsticks jumped *you* in the pitch-black.   5

**JOE** Would I heck!

**GABZ** And squeezed their mitts round your neck. Covered your eyes.

**MRS PRESLEY** I might have known: Sam Sullivan.   10

**SAM** Nah. I didn't grab her. Just whispered a few sweet nothings.

**GABZ** *'Die! Die! Die!'*, Miss.

**MRS PRESLEY** I beg your pardon, Gabrielle?

**GABZ** That's what the greasy muppet whispered to me.   15

**MR YOUNG** Oh, I say. Quite unnecessary, lads. Not kind.

**JACKY** Gabz is shaking like a jelly thigh now.

**SAM** Shaking? *Ooooh*. Then maybe that Cold Lady ghosty's swirling about again. (*pointing behind everyone*) Oh, there she goes! 20

> *Donz and Mel shriek.*

**NAT** Don't say that.

**GABZ** Forget the Cold Lady. It was you, Sully. I'd recognise the stink of your rat breath in my ear anywhere. 25

**SAM** You're gonna be sorry you said that, girl.

**GABZ** Whoooo. I'm quaking now.

**SAM** Should be. Better be. (*pause*) Ho, Joe. Got rat breath?

**JOE** No way! 30

**SAM** Have *I*?

**JOE** What?

**SAM** Rat breath.

**JOE** Duh. Dunno how rat breath smells, do I?

> *Sam breathes into Joe's face.*

**JOE** Yours is more kind of … 35

**SAM** What?

**JOE** Kinda fishy?

**GABZ, JACKY AND SAM** Fishy!

**SAM** You're gonna be sorry you said that and all. Fishy! 40

| | |
|---|---|
| **MRS PRESLEY** | Settle! What did I say about behaviour and fighting? |
| **DONZ** | Miss! *Miss!* |
| **MRS PRESLEY** | Anyone? |
| **MR YOUNG** | *Ahem*, our guide's waiting. (*nods towards the inside of the chamber*) Shouldn't we perhaps – |
| **MRS PRESLEY** | Thank you, Mr Young. When I'm good and ready. Sam, behaviour? |
| **SAM** | What about it? |
| **MRS PRESLEY** | Well, if you can't remember, you can stand there till you do. In the doorway. Don't budge. |
| **SAM** | Here? |
| **MRS PRESLEY** | Doorway. But away from everyone else – |
| **GABZ** | So we can't smell your stinking rat breath/ |
| **MRS PRESLEY** | /So there'll be no more silly attempted choking pranks that aren't funny to begin with. |

> *Mrs Presley herds everyone, except Sam, to the centre of the chamber where the Guide is waiting.*

| | |
|---|---|
| **GABZ** | Dropped my torch and all, thanks to Ratty Breath jumping me. Look. (*flicks the switch of the torch a few times*) Dud. |
| **MRS PRESLEY** | Oh, give me strength. (*to the Guide*) Another light gone, I'm afraid. |
| **GUIDE** | Unfortunate. |
| **MRS PRESLEY** | Very. Actually, it's so dark now that I'm thinking it's probably unsafe to – |

*Line numbers in right margin: 45, 50, 55, 60, 65*

GUIDE Everything's safe so long as you follow me –

TONE I said that's what she said.

JOE (*mimicking Tone*) Said that's what she said.

GUIDE – stay together and keep calm.

MRS PRESLEY Some of the group find that difficult, I'm afraid. 70

GUIDE Yes. Only one managed to follow me from the last chamber.

MRS PRESLEY Actually, it's keeping calm that's becoming the problem. These stories of yours – 75

MR YOUNG Quite fascinating, I must say.

MRS PRESLEY *Thank you*, Mr Young. These stories are disturbing the more giddy –

DONZ No way, Miss! This room's all wavy shadows.

MEL Up the walls. 80

MRS PRESLEY See what I mean? Giddy.

NAT Look like stringy bodies. Swaying.

GABZ AND JACKY *Whooooooo.* Swaying.

*Gabz and Jacky dance and wave their arms
about to throw shadows on the wall.*

MEL Shurrup!

LEE Calm down. Just *our* shadows in the lantern- 85
light again.

DEZ Sure?

MEL Cos it looks likes there's more shapes than people to me.

| JACKY | Whoo! Shadow party. Freak out! | 90 |

MR YOUNG   I say. You're quite right, Melanie.

LEE   Yeah, but it's just angles and shadows making it seem like there's extra bodies. An optical illusion.

DONZ   You're dead smart, Lee, but better not say stuff like that. 95

NAT   About extra bodies.

MRS PRESLEY   (*to Guide*) If you wouldn't mind focusing less on all this … super … para–

MR YOUNG   Paranormal? 10

MRS PRESLEY   Nonsense. Para-nonsense. (*to the Guide*) These giddy girls are becoming quite hysterical –

MEL   More than quite. I'm just gonna to stand near the door with Sam.

JOE   Worried you might hear more tapping? 10

MRS PRESLEY   – because of your stories, I'm afraid.

*A pause. The Guide looks around the chamber.*

GUIDE   They're not *my* stories.

*The Guide faces Mrs Presley and gives another sudden burst of giggling.*

*\* The pupils react by looking from the Guide to each other with character-appropriate glances and gestures.*

MRS PRESLEY   (*snappy*) But *you're* telling them. And putting unsettling pictures and ideas into my pupils' heads. 11

94

**GUIDE** What happens once people hear what I say is not my fault. I can't control what people *think*. I'm only a guide.

*A brief, tense silence descends on the group.*

**LEE** So what happened in here?

**TONE** (*animated*) Did more people die? There more 115 ghosts? When you see all those shadows it looks like there's loads of people, twisting and wriggling and reaching and –

*Joe creeps up beind Donz.*

**JOE** Boo!

*Donz yelps.*

**MRS PRESLEY** Settle! 120

**DONZ** (*panting*) But, Miss. I totally thought someone was reaching for me through the wall like Tone said.

**TONE** (*sniffs*) Anyone smelling meat?

**JOE** Meat? 125

**TONE** Like raw.

**GUIDE** (*to Tone*) You smell raw meat?

**TONE** Off raw meat.

**JACKY** (*to Tone*) Who rattled your cage?

**GUIDE** Interesting. 130

**TONE** Like when it's been sitting out for too long. Rotting. Going bad.

**SAM** With flies crawling on it?

**TONE** Yeah.

NAT Cheers. 13

DEZ So in here? People? Did they? Die?

SAM Die! Die! Die!

MEL Please, please, please don't say it was something horrible.

SAM (*in horror-movie voice*) *It was something horrible.* 14

MEL Shurrup!

GABZ Moron.

MRS PRESLEY Settle. Really, we should just finish up –

GUIDE You want to finish the tour?

MEL (*to Mrs Presley*) Can we? 14

SAM Suits me.

LEE No way.

TONE No! I want to know what happened in here first.

GUIDE It would be a pity to stop so close to the end. 15 Especially in this chamber.

DEZ How?

MRS PRESLEY (*to Dez*) *Why?*

GUIDE (*to Mrs Presley*) Good question.

DONZ Gold star to you, Miss. 15

GUIDE Because its history remains a mystery.

LEE Hey. Rhyme.

JOE (*mimicking Lee*) *Hey. Rhyme.*

TONE He was only saying, all right?

JOE Who asked you? 16

TONE  Lay off Lee, Morrison.

LEE  It's all right, Tone. Stay cool.

JACKY  Someone's deffo rattled his cage.

MRS PRESLEY  Anthony! Settle.

MR YOUNG  So this chamber? What are we looking at?  165

GUIDE  What are *you* looking at?

GABZ  Another crumbly pile of zero.

MRS PRESLEY  Can't see anything, myself. These torches are
hopeless. Really it's far too dark –

MR YOUNG  Thank you, Mrs Presley!  170

MRS PRESLEY  I beg your pardon?

MR YOUNG  You've reminded me.

> *Mr Young digs in his anorak pocket, produces
> an elasticated head torch and puts it on. Sam,
> Joe, Gabz, Jacky, Dez, Nat and Donz laugh
> and point. Lee, Mel and Tone look impressed.
> Mrs Presley doesn't know how to react or what
> to say. A smiling Mr Young turns his beam on
> everyone, dazzling them one by one so they
> cover their eyes and flinch from the light. Only
> the Guide meets the beam eye to eye.*

LEE  That's brighter than any of our torches that, Sir.

MRS PRESLEY  We could all do with one of them. (*to Mr
Young*) And we could certainly have done with  175
yours sooner.

TONE  I can see much better now.

GABZ  Flipping blinding me!

| | |
|---|---|
| JACKY | D'you mind not pointing it right in my face? |
| MRS PRESLEY | Quite. |
| MR YOUNG | Now, what am I looking for? Aha. |
| DEZ | What? See a spook, Sir? |
| MR YOUNG | Can't say I do, but this chamber is far from empty. |
| MRS PRESLEY | It is? |
| DONZ | Miss! |
| GUIDE AND MR YOUNG | Far from empty. |
| MR YOUNG | May I? Hmmm. |

*Mr Young paces the chamber, exploring the walls. Lee, Dez and Tone follow him, interested. Joe, Gabz, Jacky and Mrs Presley remain in the centre of chamber with the Guide. Sam is still in the doorway. Mel hovers nearby as does Nat. Donz flits between all the groups.*

| | |
|---|---|
| MR YOUNG | Not every day I get the chance to do a spot of subterranean archaeological sleuthing. Oh, I say! |
| DEZ | What? |
| TONE | Yeah, what? |
| MR YOUNG | High on the wall. |
| LEE | Metal ring, is that? |
| TONE | It's rusty. Aw, there's two. |
| DEZ | And is that a bit of chain? |
| DONZ | Miss, look. Rusty old rings in that wall, Miss. |
| MRS PRESLEY | (*flat*) Rusty old rings. |

**SAM** (*sarcastic*) Whoopee!      200

**TONE** (*excited*) Bet ya people got hunged there.

**MRS PRESLEY** *Hanged*, Anthony.

**GUIDE** You think?

**TONE** Look. Right height.

> *Tone stretches to the rings. Joe makes chimp noises.*

**MEL** Check out those shadows round Mr Young's      205
light.

**NAT** Look like arms trying to grab at him.

**TONE** Nah. Look like arms dangling. Twisting. Like
down from the rings.

> *Tone demonstrates.*

**JOE** (*chimp-style*) Ooooh-ooooh-ooooh.      210

**MEL** No. Just waving about.

**TONE** Dangling. See.

**NAT** Stop it.

**SAM** Stop what, shriek queen? Mr Young's torch
is throwing shapes, that's all. This place is      215
messing with your head.

**MR YOUNG** What were the rings for, I wonder?

**GUIDE** (*indicating Tone*) Well, this visitor has already –

**TONE** Hey, another ring.

**LEE** Oh yeah. It's bigger. Look, on the ceiling.      220

**DEZ** Are those score marks?

**LEE** Wow! All the way down the wall. And along
the floor.

| | |
|---|---|
| **MR YOUNG** | Scuffing, I'd say. |
| **JOE** | Nah, just dirt, that. |
| **TONE** | Like heels digging into the ground. |
| **LEE** | Whoa. Up there. Cross shapes scraped out. Sir, can you maybe shine your head – |
| **MR YOUNG** | Oh, I say. Crosses indeed. No! That's more like one of those – |
| **LEE, MR YOUNG AND GUIDE** | Pentangles. |
| **MRS PRESLEY** | For goodness' sake, whatever next? |
| **GUIDE** | Yes. Pentangles. |
| **TONE** | Pen-whats? |
| **GUIDE** | There are several scraped out in this chamber … (*points*) There. There. Here. |
| **TONE** | All near the wall rings. |
| **LEE** | Oh yeah! |
| **DONZ** | Miss! |
| **MR YOUNG** | I say. |
| **JOE** | Hang on. Pentangle whatsits. They not something to do with … |
| **JOE AND GUIDE** | Witchcraft. |
| **GUIDE** | Yes. |
| **NAT, DONZ, MEL AND MRS PRESLEY** | What! |
| **MR YOUNG** | And could these be initials scratched out? |
| **MRS PRESLEY** | That head-torch is certainly coming in handy, Mr Young. |
| **LEE** | Yeah. Look. Letters. |

TONE  M. B.                                                    **250**

SAM  Putting in some reading practice there, chimp.

TONE  I can read! You saying I can't read?

MRS PRESLEY  Calm down, Anthony.

JACKY  Where?

*Jacky and Gabz join the explorers.*

LEE  You should be a detective, Sir.                         **255**

MR YOUNG  Wouldn't that be marvellous!

SAM  (*low*) You'd make a better detective than a
teacher. (*pause*) Sherlock Youngy with his
faithful sidekick Slow Tone Watson.

MRS PRESLEY  I heard that, Sam Sullivan. And it wasn't clever  **260**
and it wasn't funny.

JACKY  Was a bit.

MR YOUNG  Could this room have been a witches' prison
of some description?

MEL  Witches!                                                **265**

JOE  (*to Gabz and Jacky*) Feel like home sweet home,
does it?

GABZ AND
JACKY  Shurrup!

MRS PRESLEY  Settle! And there's no such thing as witches.

SAM  (*pointing at Gabz and Jacky*) Er …           **270**

GABZ AND
JACKY  Shurrup!

GUIDE  Many people through the ages would dispute
that claim.

TONE  What does that mean?

| | | |
|---|---|---|
| **MRS PRESLEY** | There's no such thing as witches. | 275 |
| **GUIDE** | But enough people believed in them to make chambers like this exist. | |
| **JOE** | Chambers like what? | |
| **GUIDE** | Torture chambers. | |
| **\*DONZ** | Miss! | 280 |
| **\*MRS PRESLEY** | Oh for the love of God! | |
| **\*TONE** | This was a torture chamber? | |
| **\*MR YOUNG** | Oh, I say! | |
| **\*LEE** | Amazing! | |
| **\*MEL** | No. It's actually really totally horrible. | 285 |
| **\*NAT** | It feels horrible in here, doesn't it? | |
| **\*DEZ** | Like, you mean, a torture chamber for witches? | |
| **\*GABZ** | No, like one for saints. | |
| **\*JACKY** | Duh! | |
| **\*LEE** | Saints got tortured. | 290 |
| **\*MR YOUNG** | They did indeed. Martyred. | |

*A horrible witchy cackle from Sam.*

| | | |
|---|---|---|
| **DONZ** | Miss? | |
| **SAM** | Hold on. Thought you said this room's *(in Guide's voice)* 'history remains a mystery'? | |
| **MRS PRESLEY** | Paying attention for once were you, Sam Sullivan? | 295 |
| **SAM** | Always, Miss. | |
| **GUIDE** | I did say that. | |

*The Guide moves around the chamber, flashing her lantern at various marks on the walls.*

GUIDE But the rings and chains and scuffmarks and
the scratches – those are made by fingers by           300
the way –

LEE No way!

GABZ How d'you know?

GUIDE From the skin and nail fragments I've found in
the wall.                                              305

MEL (*mouthing to Lee*) *Found?*

GUIDE And the crosses and the pentangles and the
messages –

DEZ Does that say (*reads*) 'In-no-cent'?

LEE (*reads*) *Death speed, O God.*                   310

TONE (*reads*) *I curse all.*

DONZ Curse! Miss!

JOE Whoa!

GUIDE – mean it's likely this was a prison and a
torture chamber.                                       315

MEL Just for witches?

GUIDE Probably all sorts of accused. Some innocent.
Some evil. Some petrified. Some mad.

> *The Guide gives another short burst of unhinged*
> *giggling, almost to herself. Mel notices and*
> *nudges Lee but he's missed the Guide's outburst.*

LEE What? (*pause*) *What?*

MEL Never mind.                                        320

SAM Some bored out their brainbox.

GUIDE My visitors tell me this room has a peculiar energy.

MRS PRESLEY *Energy?*

GUIDE Electric, visitors say.                                    325

SAM *Bzzzzzzz.*

MRS PRESLEY Wish it was.

GUIDE It makes some visitors angry. Aggressive.

> *Lee and Dez nudge each other and nod at Tone.*
> *At the same time, the Guide swings her lantern*
> *on Tone and gives a brief, high-pitched snigger.*
> *Only Mel notices.*

TONE (*to Lee and Dez*) What you looking at?

GUIDE Other visitors experience a sense of someone      330
looming over them. Coiled. Ready to pounce.

JOE Pounce like attack?

DONZ Miss!

SAM (*sing-song voice*) *I'm behind you.*

DEZ Do they ever see –                                          335

> *Dez's question is interrupted by a howl from Joe*
> *that makes Mel drop her torch. It goes out.*

MR YOUNG I say, are you all –

> *Joe is lying on his back. Mr Young is the first to*
> *help him rise.*

MR YOUNG Give him air.

MRS PRESLEY Don't waste your time. He's just being silly,
acting the goat … as usual. Up you get for
goodness' sake, Joseph, you daft lump!        340

MR YOUNG  He's not pretending, Morag. He's fainted.

SAM  Joe would never faint. He fell.

DEZ  How'd that just suddenly happen?

MEL  Better not be tripping over those murdered
kids! **345**

NAT  Cos that would mean they'd followed us.

DONZ  Shurrup!

*Mr Young and Mrs Presley help Joe to stand.*

MR YOUNG  There's a fellow. You're all right.

MRS PRESLEY  Can you stand?

TONE  He's gasping. **350**

DONZ  Better get him out, Miss.

MRS PRESLEY  Are you dizzy?

NAT  He needs fresh air. I'll take him.

DEZ  How's he going to climb that ladder?

*As everyone crowds Joe, he begins to struggle
in the teachers' grip, thrashing about to look
behind him, eyes goggling.*

JOE  (*breathless*) Kicked my back in. **355**

DEZ  Who?/

SAM  /What?

MR YOUNG  You're fine now. Still a little dizzy perhaps.

JOE  Not dizzy. Winded. Two feet – booted smack
in the small of my – ow! Throbbing. **360**

GABZ  Gibbering.

MRS PRESLEY  Calm down now.

JOE   Chop-kicked my flipping kidneys.

JACKY   What's he on about?

*Joe is tearing at the back of his top.*

GABZ   Oooh. Stripteaser geezer! He's lost the plot.   365

*Gabz and Jacky wolf-whistle.*

SAM   Quit it!

JOE   Is there a mark on me?

MR YOUNG   Have you injured your back?

MEL   Someone kicked him, he said.

JOE   More than kicked.   370

GUIDE   In the small of your back?

MR YOUNG   My goodness, there are marks. Look.

MRS PRESLEY   I'd say that's the reflection of your torch-beam on his skin, Mr Young.

TONE   Aren't they shaped like footprints?   375

JOE AND GUIDE   Footprints?

*A pause.*

JOE   (*angry*) Oh, right. That's it.

MRS PRESLEY   That *is* it. You were warned, Sam Sullivan.

*Joe is hyperventilating and twisting and turning, looking about and behind him.*

MRS PRESLEY   Look at the state he's in. He's supposed to be your friend.   380

SAM   (*from the doorway to the chamber*) I never went near him! I wouldn't do that.

GABZ   Said he was gonna be sorry. Fish-breath, remember?

SAM Joe, straight up. I never touched you, mate. 385

JOE It felt like bare feet –

GUIDE Bare feet.

*The Guide sniggers to herself.*

JOE – thumping into me.

SAM I never went near –

MEL True, Miss. I've been here beside him, Miss. 390
And if Joe's going, I'm going too, by the way.

JACKY Why?

MEL Had enough, haven't I?

GABZ Not enough of Joe, though.

SAM I saw him fall. On the deck. Doof. 395

MEL I saw that too.

JOE (*panicky*) Something kicked me. Really hard.
*Really* hard.

MRS PRESLEY (*to Mr Young*) I'll need to take him out.

DONZ I'm coming with you. 400

NAT And me.

MRS PRESLEY Deep breaths, Joe. (*to the Guide*) The quickest
exit, please? And preferably not back up the
ladder.

GUIDE That's the way I would go. 405

MRS PRESLEY There must be an emergency exit. If there
isn't, I'll be on to Health and Safety soon
as I'm out of here, reporting this place for
inadequate –

| | |
|---|---|
| **MR YOUNG** | Are we all going? Because I don't think our tour's quite – |
| **MRS PRESLEY** | Actually, I'll be on to Health and Safety regardless. (*grumbling to herself*) No lighting, dangerous underfoot, poor air quality … / |
| **GUIDE** | /(*to Mr Young*) It's not. There's one final chamber. |
| **JOE** | I can't stay, I can't stay, I can't stay … |
| **DONZ** | Miss, he's away, Miss. Look, Miss. Lost it. See him, Miss. He's flapping like a maddo. |
| **MRS PRESLEY** | I see that, Donna. Thank you. (*to Joe*) Calm down, boy! (*to the Guide*) Exit? |

*The Guide passes her lantern over the group.*

| | |
|---|---|
| **GUIDE** | So are you all leaving? |
| **JOE** | I can't stay down here, I really can't – |
| **GUIDE** | For some of you the final chamber could be the most – |
| **MRS PRESLEY** | (*impatient*) Exit? |
| **LEE** | Miss, I'd like to see the final chamber. |
| **MR YOUNG** | I'd rather like that too/ |
| **MRS PRESLEY** | /*Thank you*, Mr Young. But I'm sure you appreciate I need to get this pupil out. |
| **NAT** | I'm out too, Miss./ |
| **DONZ** | /I'm coming./ |
| **MEL** | /Can we all go?/ |
| **SAM** | /Am I coming?/ |
| **JOE** | /Gotta get me out of here./ |

SAM /Miss? Am I coming? I'll behave.

MRS PRESLEY For goodness' sake. (*to Sam*) You never behave.
No. You stay put.

MR YOUNG (*to Sam*) Yes. With me. And anyone who wants
to finish the tour. 440

GUIDE Only one more chamber.

LEE I'm in.

MRS PRESLEY (*to the Guide*) Exit?

DEZ Tone?

TONE What? 445

LEE Tone's coming with us, Sir.

JOE I need out!

MRS PRESLEY EXIT!

GUIDE There.

> *The Guide holds up her lantern to reveal an
> emergency exit in the corridor, just outside the
> doorway to the chamber.*

MRS PRESLEY Did we see that before? 450

GUIDE Were you looking before?

MRS PRESLEY That should have been pointed out to us
earlier. And it should be properly marked.

DONZ Exit, Miss. Halleluiah.

> *Donz and Mel push the door open. Strip lights
> flood a concrete staircase. With a cheer, Joe,
> Mel, Donz and Nat belt up the stairs.*

MRS PRESLEY Walk! *Walk, Milton Street!* Wait for me at the 455
top!

> *Sam starts following.*

**MRS PRESLEY** Where d'you think you're going?

**MR YOUNG** You stay with me.

**GUIDE** (*smiling at Sam*) Stay for the last chamber.

**SAM** How? 46

**JACKY** I'll stay with you, Sam.

**MR YOUNG** Mrs Presley needs to take care of Joe, that's how.

**MRS PRESLEY** *Why*, not how. (*sincere and with relief*) But thank you, Mr Young. See you shortly. 46

**SAM** (*aside*) Not if I see you first. And don't call me shortly.

**MRS PRESLEY** I heard that, Sam Sullivan. And for heaven's sake try not to do anything daft for once in your life. 47

> *Exit Mrs Presley, closing the door so the remaining group is in near darkness again.*

**GUIDE** So, the Final Chamber?

**GABZ** (*nervous*) I should have left.

**SAM** You don't want to see 'the final chamber'. With me?

**GABZ** Er, let me think.(*pause*) Not really. 47

**SAM** Cheers.

**GABZ** Just gonna be another stupid dark room. (*to Guide*) Innit?

**GUIDE** Follow me and you'll find out.

> *Blackout.*

# Scene Eight

## To the Final Chamber

*Mr Young, Sam, Gabz, Jacky, Lee, Tone and Dez
follow the Guide down a narrow passageway. Dez
and Tone are at the rear and Dez keeps looking
over his shoulder.*

DEZ  We not nearly there?

GUIDE  Yes.

DEZ  And haven't we walked miles from that exit?

GUIDE  Yes.

GABZ  Feels like miles.                                    5

TONE  All right, Dez?

JACKY  Yeah, Dezzo, what's with the creepy heavy
breathing down my neck? If it's cos you like
being close to me in the dark and you're
getting ideas, forget it.                                 10

DEZ  (*to Jacky*) What? (*to Mr Young*) Sir, see, if the rest
of our lights go out, how'd we get back?

*Mr Young doesn't hear Dez's question as he's
busy trying to catch up with the Guide and get
her attention.*

SAM  (*to Dez*) Dur, the Guide.

**DEZ** But what if *she* can't see? Would we not end up wandering about? 15

**JACKY** For totally ever and ever?/

**DEZ** /Cos did she not say these tunnels are a maze?/

**TONE** /Warren./

**SAM** /End up wandering about for ever and 20 ever and ever and ever with the Cold Lady and the cobbler and his dead kids and the witches till you die yourself. End up haunting groups like us. Blowing cold air at hot chicks. *Whoooooooo!* 25

**JACKY** Quit./

**GABZ** /Shurrup.

**SAM** Imagine meeting the ghosts of you two hagettes. Grizzly.

> *Dez falls back.*

**DEZ** Sir? 30

**LEE** Dez has a quez.

**GABZ** Ha ha. Look. Youngy's too busy boring Spooky to death.

**DEZ** *Sir?*

**MR YOUNG** (*to the Guide*) … if you were ever looking for a 35 guide yourself on a hike up the fells we could perhaps exchange … Desmond? Are you all right?

**DEZ** (*gesturing back to where they've come from*) Sir, see that exit? That the others went up? 40

*Mr Young tries to point his head-torch in the direction Dez is indicating.*

MR YOUNG  Well. Now, I'm not sure if I can actually …

GABZ  Don't think he means, like, can you, like, *literally* see it.

JACKY  Considering it's miles back.

LEE AND GUIDE  Hardly.                                                        45

DEZ  Sir, would it be OK if I just nip up it too?

MR YOUNG  Actually … well … and what about the final chamber?

GUIDE  We're almost there.

DEZ  Can I, Sir?                                                              50

MR YOUNG  I really can't let you wander along these passages on your –

SAM  I'll go with him.

GABZ  Elvis says you're staying down here, Sully.

MR YOUNG  Yes. So it's best we … I mean, *you* do what Mrs  55
Presley instructed.

SAM  But you're in charge too. Elvis said. So you can call the shots.

MR YOUNG  Yes, but Mrs Presley's already instructed you to stay –                                                               60

DEZ  Did you hear her say *I* had to stay down here, Sir?/

SAM  Un-instruct me then, Sir. Go on.

DEZ  Sir?

SAM  You can do it, Sir.                                                     65

DEZ  I'm feeling a bit funny, see?

MR YOUNG  Funny?

SAM  Funny scared? Eh? Eh? Eh?

DEZ  So can I? Go?

MR YOUNG  Not on your own.                                    70

JACKY  I'll go with him. So long as you give me a
torch.

GABZ  Then what do *we* do?

MR YOUNG  If you must go up, we'll all have to.

LEE AND GUIDE  And miss the final chamber?                    75

MR YOUNG  I'm sorry, but what can I –

DEZ  Sir, can I not just sprint it?

JACKY  I'll run with you. And we'll hold hands. Be like
we're in *The Great Escape*.

GABZ  (*to Jacky*) What are you like? Anything with a        80
pulse.

DEZ  Eh?

MR YOUNG  But how will I know you've made it safely to
the exit?

SAM  You'll know they didn't if you never see them          85
again.

MR YOUNG  Do you mind if I say that wouldn't be your
most helpful comment of the day, Sam?

SAM  And you end up in the middle of this massive
investigation. Head teach' and cops and that.          90
And you have to stand up in court and swear
on the Bible 'bout how you totally said Dez

and Jacky could just try to find their own
way out then they went and disappeared
so you lose your job and get sent down to a          95
maximum-security penitentiary and stuck in
a cell with a psycho serial killer with a grudge
against teachers!

MR YOUNG    (*to Guide*) I'm sorry, but if Desmond leaves,
we'll all have to –          100

LEE AND TONE    Aw!

LEE    What if they sing, Sir?

MR YOUNG, DEZ, JACKY AND GABZ    Sing?

LEE    'Stop the Bus', till they reach the exit. So long
as they keep singing, you know they're sound.          105

MR YOUNG    Lee, that's rather a good idea./

SAM    /(*shaking his head*) Uh-uh. Have you actually
*heard* Jacky singing? Rather be haunted by
the Cold Lady.

DEZ    But what happens if we stop singing?          110

JACKY    (*to Sam*) Eh, d'you mind? I'm a lovely singer!

MR YOUNG    Well … well …

SAM    (*to Gabz*) Eh, play yourself back sometime.

TONE    Then we all charge out to find you.

DEZ    (*panicky*) Can I just go? (*to the Guide*) What          115
way?

GUIDE    Follow this wall till you reach the door. And
don't go into any of the chambers by yourself.

JACKY    No danger.

SAM  Why not?      120

GUIDE  It would be most foolish.

SAM  Why?

MR YOUNG  All right. All out. That's it.

LEE  That's rubbish.

GUIDE  Yes. It's always unfortunate when my visitors  125
miss the final chamber.

MR YOUNG  I'm afraid we must.

> *The Guide's gaze falls on Sam while she*
> *considers this remark.*

GUIDE  (*to Dez*) In that case, follow me. Quickly.

DEZ  You're taking us out?

JACKY  Me too.      130

GUIDE  Quickly. The rest of you stay here.

> *Exit the Guide followed by Dez and Jacky.*

LEE AND TONE  (*calling out to Dez and Jacky*) Sing!

TONE  She better be coming back with that light.
Don't fancy my chances with this. (*shakes his*
*torch*)      13

GABZ  She better be coming back full stop.

> *Voices of Dez and Jacky singing a couple*
> *of tuneless, wobbly loops of 'Stop the Bus'*
> *gradually fade, until a reassuring metallic clang*
> *is heard. The remaining group stand in silence.*

LEE  Is that her coming back?

TONE  No footsteps.

GABZ Why didn't I quit with Jacky? Bet she's never
coming back. 140

SAM Boo-hoo.

> *With a high-pitched manic giggle, the Guide
> suddenly reappears, lantern raised. Everyone in
> the group registers shock/surprise.*

GUIDE Now.

LEE Whoa. How d'you do that?

SAM It was freaky.

MR YOUNG I say, you seemed to appear out of nowhere. 145

GUIDE Did I? (*pause*) So, the final chamber.

> *Blackout.*

# Scene Nine

## Office of Hidden City Tours

*Virtual darkness. Donz, Nat, Mel and Joe are groping and stumbling around, using their mobiles for light and trying to find signals on them.*

**DONZ** Dead.

**MEL** As all the spooks and spirits down …
(*shudders*) What was that *like*?

**NAT** Stop!

*Mrs Presley is trying to use the normal telephone in the office.*

**MRS PRESLEY** … educationally and historically interesting or 5
not, I most certainly won't be recommending
this half-cocked operation to anyone in a
hurry. (*slams the phone receiver down and takes
out her own mobile*)

**JOE** Elvis just said *c*– 10

**MRS PRESLEY** Of course I didn't, Joseph Morrison. And don't
you bother saying it either.

**NAT** You so did, Miss.

**DONZ** Heard you, Miss. Half-cocked, Miss.

**MEL** Actually did, Miss. 15

**118**

**MRS PRESLEY** Actually I didn't. Although right now I feel like saying plenty worse.

**DONZ** Oh! You mean like say rude words, Miss? (*gasps*) You don't let *us* say rude words.

**MRS PRESLEY** The word I used isn't a rude word anyway. 20

**DONZ** Sure about that, Miss?

**MRS PRESLEY** Quite sure. It's a shooting term, Donna.

**JOE** Still got the word *c–*

**MRS PRESLEY** (*cutting in very quickly*) A word with several senses. Another sense being a male hen, 25 from which the phrase 'cock of the walk', as in strutting and bold, is derived. Which is what I'm delighted to see you're back to being, Joseph. Now you appear to have miraculously recovered from your subterranean attack of 30 the vapours.

**NAT** Huh?

**JOE** Nothing mysterious about it. Totally pole-axed down there, so I was.

**MEL** He was too. 35

*Dez and Jacky enter, in a rush via the emergency door inside the office.*

**JACKY** Calm it, Dez. We're up.

**MRS PRESLEY** Finally. Home time.

**NAT** Burger time, Miss!

*Nat hurries to the main door of office, which is closed.*

119

**JOE** Double burger time. Sauce and fries!

**NAT** And jumbo coke. 40

**MRS PRESLEY** Definitely must be recovered from your attack of the vapours. And it's bus time, not burger time … (*waves her mobile about*) as soon as I get a blasted signal. (*to Dez and Jacky*) The others at your back I take it? 45

**NAT** Hey, Miss. This door's totally jammed.

**DEZ** (*to Mrs Presley*) Just came up with Jacky, didn't I? (*to Jacky*) Had enough, hadn't you?

**JACKY** Er, enough of you. I wasn't the one throwing the big girl's wobbly. 50

**DEZ** Me? Wobbly? (*to Nat*) How d'you mean jammed?

**NAT** As in, like, not opening.

**MRS PRESLEY** (*trying the door*) Of course it's opening. (*pause*) Oh. 55

**DONZ** Like she said, Miss. It's not opening.

**JACKY** (*doing a panting imitation of Dez*) 'Where's the exit, Sir? Can I go up?' That's what you were like.

**MRS PRESLEY** (*tugging the door*) Oh, for goodness' sake. How did that happen? 60

**JOE** Why you automatically look at me? Would I lock myself in this dumpster when I'm gagging for a burger?

**DONZ** Miss! We're trapped. (*bangs on the main door*) Help! Help! (*to Nat*) Don't just stand there. 65

**DONZ AND NAT** Help! Help!

JACKY  Aw, shurrup. It's like listening to two loonies who can't sing auditioning for *X Factor*.

MEL  No one's gonna hear anyway. Down at the bottom of an alley, 'member?  70

DONZ  So we could be trapped all night?

DONZ AND NAT  *Help! Help!*

MRS PRESLEY  Don't be ridiculous, Donna.

DONZ  But, Miss, we're locked in, Miss.

DEZ  Not really, eh?  75

NAT  Better not be. I'm dying of hunger.

JACKY  Don't look it.

NAT  Are you calling me fat?

JACKY  Never!

NAT  Sounded like you were to me, missy.  80

MRS PRESLEY  Settle!

MEL  Why'd that door be locked now anyway? (*pause*) You know what?

DEZ AND DONZ  What?

*A pause.*

MEL  Something about tonight just feels …  85

DEZ  What?

MEL  I don't know. (*pause*) Just not right.

MRS PRESLEY  You can say that again. And not just something.

JOE  (*creepy voice*) Everything feels not right.  90

MRS PRESLEY  And that's why I'm trying to get us done and home.

**DEZ** How? Like since we're locked in?

**NAT** And the phones don't work.

*****DONZ** Miss, how will we get … /   95

*****NAT** /I'm so, so starving./

*****DEZ** /We really gonna be stuck here all night?/

*****MEL** /No way!/

*****JACKY** /Better blooming not be./

*****JOE** /Say that again.   10●

**MRS PRESLEY** Settle! Yapping and whining and whinging at me like a class of starving kittens won't help! I can't hear myself *think*.

**JOE** Sorree.

**MRS PRESLEY** First things first. Only half of us are present.   10●

**JOE** Not me. I'm all here, Miss. Every bit of me.

**MRS PRESLEY** So we're going nowhere till we're all together. I must say, I'm surprised Mr Young let you pair just wander back out on your own.

**JACKY** He didn't. He was all for leaving too. Then the   11●
Lady of the Lamp showed us out instead.

**DEZ** But Mr Y wanted to stay for the final chamber, didn't he?

**JACKY** Dunno why. Following that guide woman? Forget your cobblers and witches, she's the   115
freakiest part of my night.

**MRS PRESLEY** Mmm … odd woman, I must say.

**MEL** Well odd.

**DEZ** Gripping my hand the whole way, wasn't she?

**DONZ, NAT, MRS PRESLEY** Who? The *Guide*?                    120

**JOE** Now that really is creepy.

**DEZ** No, I mean Jacky!

**JACKY** Er … other way round, wimpster.

**DEZ** Are you sure she didn't speak a word?

**JACKY** Just sorta … kinda … glided ahead.         125

**JOE** Glided?

**JACKY** Stopped when she came to the door. Pointed
at the bar we'd to push.

**JOE** (*as Guide*) 'Push that bar.'

**JACKY** No. She never spoke to us.                   130

**DEZ** Just pointed.

**JACKY** Then kinda …

**DONZ, NAT AND MEL** Kinda what?

**JACKY** Just kinda sorta …

**DEZ** Melted.                                         135

**DONZ, MEL, NAT, JOE AND MRS PRESLEY** *Melted?*

**JACKY** Yeah. Like the dark was kinda –

**MEL** What?

**DEZ** Swallowing her.

**DONZ, MEL, NAT, JOE AND MRS PRESLEY** Swallowing?    140

**JOE** Speaking of swallowing, could still murder
that burger. So how's about I bust this lock
and we boost, Miss?

**MRS PRESLEY** No thank you.

**JOE** Clean and easy. I know what I'm doing. 14·

**JACKY** He does too. I've seen him in action.

**MRS PRESLEY** I'm quite confident you do, Joe. Probably get an A-star in lock-busting, but I'd rather find a solution to our predicament that didn't involve unnecessary property damage. 15·

*Mrs Presley takes out Dez's phone and stands at the jammed door trying to get a signal.*

**DEZ** Hey, going to give us that back now, Miss?

**MRS PRESLEY** Oh, for goodness' sake! I'm sure I had two bars there.

**DONZ** A signal?

**MRS PRESLEY** Not any more. 155

**DEZ** So who's the dude with the top Milton Street gadg? Want me to show you the ace pics it takes too?

**MRS PRESLEY** Just a minute, Desmond!

*Mrs Presley is pressed against the main door, angling Dez's phone to find a signal. From the other side comes a sudden rattle of a key. Mrs Presley yelps and leaps back as the door opens to reveal a harassed-looking man. According to his badge, he is 'Gordon: Official Hidden City Tour Guide'. Gordon is equally startled to find Mrs Presley against the door.*

**GORDON AND MRS PRESLEY** For goodness' sake … What's going …? 16·

**DEZ** (*taking his mobile back*) Finished, Miss?

**DONZ** Free at last!

*Headed by Donz and Joe, the pupils attempt an
escape.*

MRS PRESLEY Oi! Get your insolent, ill-disciplined carcasses
back here immediately!

*The pupils return.*

NAT But, Miss, I'm so starved.                                          165

*Gordon flicks a switch that floods the office with
light. He produces head-torches, hand-held
torches, maps and a clipboard from his desk*

GORDON (*to Mrs Presley*) Now I've no idea how you got
in here, but I take it you're my eight p.m. party.

JOE (*aside*) Not your nothing, sunshine.

GORDON (*consulting clipboard*) Milton Street School?

JOE AND JACKY Milton Street Massive, yo!                                170

MRS PRESLEY And you are?

GORDON Apart from very late, and very sorry, I'm
Gordon, your guide. I'm surprised you're all
still here, to tell the truth.

DEZ (*to Mel*) What's with all the kit, d'you think?                    175

MEL Must be another tour starting.

GORDON Although you shouldn't really be on these
premises. Health and safety protocol and all
that.

MRS PRESLEY *Health and safety?* Puh! Don't make me laugh.             180

GORDON These minors can't be on the property
unsupervised.

MRS PRESLEY But *I'm* supervising them.

JACKY  And I'm not a miner, thank you very much.

GORDON  Actually in this location, madam, you'd be                    18
unauthorised.

MRS PRESLEY  Actually, I think you'll find I'm fully authorised.
Considering these pupils are in my charge.

GORDON  Actually, you'll find you're not. According to
the official council health and safety policy         19
– which by the way, I'll be asking you to read
and sign before we begin our tour proper –

JACKY  (*aside to Joe*) Er, if he thinks we're taking
another trip down Nightmare Alley –

JOE  – he can stuff his thoughts up his –/              19

GORDON  /– members of the general public are only
permitted access to these premises when
accompanied by the official guide. Which is
Yours Truly.

MRS PRESLEY  But how can you supervise when you're not     20
physically present?

DEZ  Yeah? How?

GORDON  Circumstances beyond my control I'm afraid.
In my defence, I *have* been trying to phone
you, (*checking clipboard*) Mrs Priestly?      20

MRS PRESLEY  Presley.

JOE  As in the King. (***Elvis voice***) A-hubba-hubba.
*Thank you very much.*

MRS PRESLEY  Are you aware there's no mobile signal on
your 'premises'?                                21

GUIDE  I assure you there is.

**DONZ** Hey, gotta signal now. Four bars.

**MEL AND NAT** (*checking their mobiles*) Same.

**GORDON** Anyway, I can only apologise. Puncture to my
rear offside. But I'm here now.                                       215

**JOE** Stump up for a burger if you're really sorry.

**GORDON** Not that sorry, sonny. (*to Mrs Presley*) No
wonder you look so unimpressed.

**JOE** (*aside*) Don't worry, Elvis' face always looks like
that.                                                                 220

**GORDON** I can't believe I've managed to be late for my
first shift myself.

**MRS PRESLEY** Well, we almost left an hour ago.

**GORDON** And I'm glad you didn't. Less of you than I
thought, mind you. Cosy little tour party, eh?           225

**MRS PRESLEY** Oh, there's others. Should be back up any
time.

**DONZ** We're the wimps and scaredy cats.

**JOE** Speak for yourself.

**GORDON** Sorry, back *up*?                                         230

**MRS PRESLEY** They're on their final chamber now.

**GORDON** What 'final chamber'?

**DONZ** Gabz and Sam and Lee and Tone.

**MRS PRESLEY** Down below. Four more pupils. With *my*
colleague, Mr Young.                                                 235

**GORDON** Down below?

**MRS PRESLEY** In the final chamber.

.

127

GORDON   What 'final chamber'? I haven't even put the corridor lights on down there. And you need maps. And a safety briefing. Those tunnels and vaults are a warren.

MRS PRESLEY   That's what your colleague … Oh, what *is* the woman's name, by the way? I couldn't get her to tell me.

GORDON   Woman?

MRS PRESLEY   She just called herself 'the Guide'.

JOE   (*creepy voice*) *The Guide.*/

GORDON   /The Guide?

MRS PRESLEY   Altogether terribly impersonal, considering she's showing a bunch of youngsters about. Funny manner. Knows her onions, mind you.

GORDON
AND JOE   Onions?

MRS PRESLEY   She was spouting non-stop supernatural nonsense down that hatch.

GORDON   *Hatch?*

JOE   Is there an echo in here? (*creepy voice*) *Supernatural nonsense down that hatch.*

MRS PRESLEY   To the underground doo-dahs. (*points to the hatch*) There. We all clambered down that death-trap.

GORDON   You can't. You shouldn't. That hatch is unsafe.

MRS PRESLEY   Tell me about it. It was a health and safety minefield. But down we trooped.

GORDON   I don't see how. It's sealed shut.

JOE  Wasn't sealed earlier. (*in the Guide's voice*) Next.   265
Next. Next. Go. Go. Go.

MEL  (*to Gordon*) That was the other guide he was
doing by the way.

NAT  Mrs Happy.

JACKY  Lady with the Lamp.   270

JOE  Scary Mary.

DONZ  (*whisper*) Hey, what if she's his wife and we're
slagging her off?

JACKY  Calling her Lady of the Lamp's hardly slagging.
Droney Weirdo with the Lamp would be   275
slagging.

NAT  Took us round all those creepy rooms.

MEL AND JACKY  (*in the Guide's voice*) Chambers.

JOE  With crappy torches.

DONZ  Then totally freaked us with stories about   280
dead people.

MEL  And draughts.

NAT  And tapping cobblers.

GORDON  *Who* did this?

MRS PRESLEY  Your colleague.   285

GORDON  But I don't have a 'colleague'.

MRS PRESLEY  The other guide then. The woman who met
us, and then sent us down that hatch.

GORDON  But I told you: it's sealed. Look.

*Gordon proves that the hatch is sealed, pointing
to a closed bolt on the top of it.*

| | | |
|---|---|---|
| **MRS PRESLEY** | Well, it was open earlier. | 29 |
| **DONZ** | We've all been down it. | |
| **MEL** | Into those spooky chambers. | |
| **GORDON** | But your tour starts here. (*Gordon opens a door*) With a safety demonstration. And a video reconstruction of the underground passages and a time-line. Then you get your torches and your flashlights and a map, and I check if anyone's worried about enclosed spaces and then I – | 29 |
| **MRS PRESLEY** | Well, your colleague skipped all that. She huddled us into chambers full of nothing but tales of ghosts and murderers and witches. Had this lot scared out their wits. | 30 |
| **JOE** | Nah. | |
| **DONZ** | Yeah! | 30 |
| **MRS PRESLEY** | They were tripping over each other and groping in the dark to boot. An accident waiting to happen, this whole shebang. I just hope she's taking care of the others. | |
| **GORDON** | The others? | 31 |
| **MRS PRESLEY** | I've told you: four pupils. | |
| **JACKY** | And Mr Young-Young. | |
| **MRS PRESLEY** | All still below with this guide you don't seem to know anything about. | |
| **GORDON** | Why would I? *I'm* the tour guide. The *only* tour guide. | 31 |

PUPILS What?

*A pause.*

MRS PRESLEY (*slowly*) So, in that case –

MEL – who –

JOE – the hell – 320

DEZ – is down there now?

*Blackout.*

# Scene Ten

## The Devil's Face

*In this scene the Guide's behaviour is unsettling and sinister. As Tone swings into the nearest doorway he clonks his head on its lintel.*

TONE  Ow!

*Mr Young also thumps his head on the lintel, catching his head-torch so it pings off and hits the wall. Gabz giggles. But then the head torch goes out.*

MR YOUNG  Oh, I say!

*Gabz isn't giggling now. The group huddles into a tiny room, with a ceiling so low that everyone has to stoop. It is very, very dark; there are just two weak torches left and the Guide's gloomy lantern. Gabz is immediately breathing hard. Sam hovers on the threshold of the chamber, not entering.*

GABZ  Yikes-crikes.

SAM  Whassup?

GABZ  Sucks in here.                                        5

LEE  Hear that dripping? Plick, plick, plick …

SAM  Bl-oo-d. Dripping down dem walls.

GABZ Shurrup!

SAM Grow up! Just another stupid old room, innit?

GABZ Shoulda left with Jacky.                                    10

SAM Too late innit, innit?

GUIDE (*to Sam*) Come right inside, please.

LEE Doesn't smell too nifty neither.

TONE Wonder what's dripping.

SAM Bl-oo-d! (*to Guide*) I'm awright, ta. Can see        15
what I see from here.

GUIDE (*to Sam*) You need to come inside.

MR YOUNG Oh, I say! It's very stale air.

GABZ Mings of sick.

TONE My bedroom stank like this one time.               20

SAM Just one time?

> *The Guide stares at Sam until he enters the*
> *chamber.*

SAM Pwah!

TONE Turned out it was the cat hiding something
he'd killed.

GABZ Stop it./                                                        25

SAM /What? Pwah! You're right, Lee. Reeks, man.

TONE Rat it was. Maybe. Too chewed-up to tell./

GABZ /Shurrup! Think there's rats? Sir? *Sir?* Think
there's rats in here?/

MR YOUNG /Well, perhaps if we could learn the history of    30
this chamber. And then quickly join the –

133

**GUIDE** I won't take long to tell you the history of this chamber.

*The Guide gives another of her manic giggles.*

**MR YOUNG** Oh.

**LEE** Why not?                                                    35

**GUIDE** It's an empty chamber.

**LEE** Swizzle.

**SAM** Empty chamber full of smell. (*gagging*) Pwah!

*The Guide swings her lantern on Sam who seems more uncomfortable than anyone else and still hovers near the chamber entrance.*

**GUIDE** In which my visitors always experience an unpleasant smell.                              40

**LEE** And is that all there is to it?

**TONE** A bad smell?

**GUIDE** That's all most of my visitors experience.

**GABZ** What's that supposed to mean?

**GUIDE** Some find the smell unbearable. And no one    45
ever feels comfortable.

**GABZ** Well, it's hardly the Hilton.

**MR YOUNG** And it's particularly foul and small.

**SAM** Like you, Gabbo.

**GABZ** What was that, Sully?                             50

**SAM** Phew! And hot.

**GABZ** That's more like it.

**MR YOUNG** Mmm. Stuffy.

**SAM** No, hot. Really hot.

**GABZ** That's just cos you're standing close to me,      55
Sully-boy.

**SAM** Puh! Ya think so?

**LEE** (*whispers*) Why make this the last room when
there's no story? Thought we'd go out with the
big finale. 'King's Chamber', maybe?      60

**GABZ** Er. King's Chamber in a stinking dunny. I don't
think so.

**LEE** S'pose not. (*pause*) Mega-swizzle this, but …

*The Guide moves her lantern from Sam's face
and holds it at arm's length and shoulder height
to a portion of the back wall. She answers Lee
without looking at him.*

**GUIDE** I brought you here to see who meets the
Devil's Face.      65

**MR YOUNG** I beg your pardon?/

**GABZ** /She just say?/

**GUIDE** /Few visitors do. But I sense …

*Another tiny private giggle from the Guide.*

**SAM** What?

**GABZ** Better flipping not be me.      70

**TONE** I just see a wall.

**LEE** Old bricks.

**GABZ** Same. So … we going?

**GUIDE** An old brick wall is all most visitors see. But
sometimes, just around …      75

*The Guide swings her lantern on Sam. His eyes
are fixed on the wall, a stricken look on his face.*

GABZ Hey, whassup Sully? Oh, lemme guess: 'the
Devil's Face'.

*Sam points at the wall with his torch and he
becomes more and more agitated as he speaks:*

SAM Nobody else …?

TONE What?

GABZ Yeah, what? 80

SAM See?

LEE See what?

SAM Those eyes staring.

TONE What eyes?

GABZ Good one. 85

SAM You don't see them? That face?

GUIDE The Devil's Face.

GABZ What face? Sir? There's no face.

MR YOUNG I don't see anything. (*pause*) And, actually, I
suspect Mrs Presley will be starting to wonder 90
if we're ever –

SAM Eyes staring right into mine. Shiny-black and
hard and –

LEE Torch reflection.

TONE Bouncing off the brick. That'll be the shine. 95

SAM And the lips are, like … moving and
muttering. Wet and twisted. Look!

GABZ All right, Sully. Wind-up's over. Sir, we gonna boost?

SAM Gawping straight at me. 100

LEE Nothing there, man.

TONE No face. Just bricks.

SAM Can you not see that face?

GABZ Sorree.

SAM Teeth. Long. Sharp./ 105

GUIDE /Sharp.

GUIDE AND SAM Uneven. Broken.

GABZ Sir, Sully's freaking me out here. Not kidding.

SAM Why's he keep staring? He won't stop staring.

GABZ Sully, this ain't funny no more. 110

SAM (*his hands over his ears, dropping his torch and retreating*) Lips whispering stuff.

TONE Who's whispering?

LEE No one. Just a draught.

MR YOUNG Quite.

SAM (*at the wall*) Quit! Leave me alone. 115

MR YOUNG Come on, Sam. Time to stop joshing, eh?

GABZ Sir, I don't think he's pretending.

GUIDE No.

SAM (*to the wall*) Stop saying that! I'm not. Leave me alone. 120

TONE Sir, get him out. He's flipped his lid.

MR YOUNG Let's all get out. Now.

GUIDE  Well, the tour *is* over.

> *Mr Young tries to herd Gabz, Lee and Tone from the chamber. Sam is staring at the wall and mumbling. And blocking the exit.*

*SAM  No. I won't. Go away. Stop!

TONE  What's he seeing?  125

GABZ  Whatever it is, it's scaring him out his box. And I don't want to know.

*SAM  Make him stop staring.

MR YOUNG  No one's there, Sam.

*SAM  There's a face on that wall. And it's bad, Sir!  130

MR YOUNG  (*sharp*) Come on, now. That's enough!

> *As Mr Young approaches, Sam lurches away and flees the chamber.*

GABZ  Sam!

TONE  He's gone!

GABZ  We can see that!

MR YOUNG
AND GABZ  Sam! Come back.  135

LEE  Sam!

GUIDE  He isn't listening. He has to run. They all run.

GABZ  Who all run?

GUIDE  (*smiling*) My visitors who see the Devil's Face.

LEE  But that wall's blank.  140

GUIDE  That boy –

GABZ  Sam.

GUIDE  – didn't think so. (*pause*) Did he?

*The Guide giggles.*

MR YOUNG Listen. This isn't funny. What way did he go? (*pause*) What way did he go?                    145

GUIDE I have no idea.

MR YOUNG Will he find his way out?

GUIDE He'll try. (*pause*) Yes. All my visitors who see the Devil's Face try to find a way out.

TONE And do they?                    150

*Silence. The Guide stares straight ahead.*

GABZ *Do* they?

*Silence. The Guide continues to stare straight ahead.*

MR YOUNG AND PUPILS SAM!

*Blackout. A faint giggle from the Guide.*

# Scene Eleven

## Office of Hidden City Tours

*Gabz, Lee and Tone enter, stumbling into the bright office via the emergency door, followed by Mr Young.*

**JOE** Yo! Let's go! Burger time!

**TONE** Proper light!

**MRS PRESLEY** Finally, Mr Young! I was thinking about sending a search party –

**TONE** Better had. 5

**MRS PRESLEY** I beg your pardon?

*Mr Young, Gabz and Lee roam the office, not paying attention to the others.*

**MR YOUNG** Sam?

**GABZ** (*upset*) Sir! He's not here.

**JOE** So how was 'the final chamber'? Bit pale there, Gabbo. Spooky-wooky, scary-wary, frighty- 10 wighty?

**LEE** Don't ask.

**DONZ** How?

**MRS PRESLEY** *Why*?

**MR YOUNG** (*urgent*) Did he come up this? (*yanks at bolted 15 hatch*)

LEE Sir, he's still down there. Has to be.

MRS PRESLEY Mr Young, where's Sam Sullivan?

GORDON I wouldn't waste energy pulling that handle, Sir. The hatch is bolted. 20

MR YOUNG Yes, I can see that, thank you. It needs to be unbolted. Immediately.

GORDON Sir, you can tug all you like. I won't be granting access down under *that* way in a month of Sundays. 25

MR YOUNG But we've already *been* down it! The … the … your … (*reading Gordon's badges*) *she* sent us!

MRS PRESLEY *Thank you*, Mr Young. I've just been through all that with this gentleman.

GORDON And all I can say at the moment is there's 30 clearly been a major security –

JOE Coc–

*Joe is silenced by a look from Mrs Presley.*

MR YOUNG Oh, I say.

MRS PRESLEY It appears that the … our … that …

JOE Freakoid, creepster, fake guide-woman. 35

MRS PRESLEY Quite. She has, in fact, nothing whatsoever to do with –

GABZ Huh?

GORDON Whoever's down below is *not* a guide, Sir. I don't know who she is. (*pause*) She's nothing. 40 No one.

**GABZ** But Mrs Presley had her swanning us underground in the dark!

**JOE** (*in Guide's voice*) *Come on now, little kiddywinks. Follow me till you're completely lost and at my mercy.* 45

**MRS PRESLEY** That was only because she seemed to know exactly what she was doing.

**MEL** (*aside*) I didn't like what she was doing.

**MRS PRESLEY** (*pointing at the door through which the Guide had entered*) She appeared from there when we arrived. 50

**JOE** She forced us down that flipping crickety-rickety ladder and all.

**MRS PRESLEY** And she told us she knew her way all round the chambers. 55

**TONE** Never checked her ID or nothing.

**MRS PRESLEY** (*weakly*) Anything.

**TONE** You not meant to check out stuff like that?

**JOE** Bet you will after this, Miss, eh? 60

**DONZ** Yeah, Miss.

**JOE** That's if you don't get the heave-ho, Miss.

**MR YOUNG** My goodness. Am I honestly hearing that we … you … we let a *stranger* –

**LEE** Could be a psycho. 65

**JOE** Sicko.

**NAT** Nutjob.

**MR YOUNG** Quite. And we let her lead a group of … *children* –

JACKY Er, hardly. 70

LEE Like a spooky Pied Piper.

MR YOUNG – through a maze of tunnels.

MEL And now one of us is lost.

MR YOUNG Sam's still down there, Morag.

MRS PRESLEY Thank you, Rupert, I – 75

GABZ Off his trolley, by the way. Lady Gaga.

LEE Gibbering that he saw the Devil's Face on a wall.

TONE Then went AWOL.

MRS PRESLEY He *what*? Went AWOL on a wall? What does 80 that even *mean*?

MR YOUNG Seems to think he saw the Devil's Face on the wall, Morag. In the last room. That … our … oh, whoever she is, she told him sometimes –

LEE – 'my visitors' – 85

MR YOUNG – see a hideous image of the … /

MR YOUNG, GABZ, LEE AND TONE Devil's Face.

TONE And Sam sawed it.

MRS PRESLEY (*weakly*) *Saw* not *sawed*, Anthony. Sam's not a carpenter. 90

DONZ, JACKY, MEL AND DEZ The Devil's Face?/

GORDON /The Devil's Face. Mmm. Now … that actually rings …

*Gordon rummages around his desk. He finds an old book and begins flicking through it.*

MRS PRESLEY   I had an instinct from the start, didn't I?

MR YOUNG   Did you?   95

MRS PRESLEY   I knew there was something fishy about that woman. Filling this lots' daft heads with supernatural drivel –

MR YOUNG   Did you really, Morag?

MRS PRESLEY   She wouldn't even tell me her name. That had   100 me wondering. A wrong 'un. Female instinct, you see.

MR YOUNG   I only wish you'd expressed your concerns sooner. I don't share your female instinct.

MEL   Kept saying we didn't like it, Miss.   105

MRS PRESLEY   And then the ridiculous tales. Devil's Face, indeed. Give me strength.

GORDON   There *is* a Devil's Face down there. Supposedly.

MRS PRESLEY   Oh, for the love of –   110

GORDON   In one of the ante-rooms I haven't put on the tour.

DEZ   Why not?

MEL   Too scary?

GORDON   No, no. Just far too long a trek to bother with.   115 Air quality's not great that deep into the vaults either. And it stinks.

TONE   Like something died?

GORDON   Still a few sewage issues to iron out in the sections we're not opening to tourists.   120

**JACKY AND GABZ** Lovely!

**GORDON** And as I recall it feels –

**DEZ** Feels what?

**MR YOUNG** Excuse me! We've a missing boy issue to sort; never mind sewage –　125

**GABZ** Loonied out, Sam was.

**GORDON** Nasty atmosphere altogether. And as I say, there *is* a story about a face … (*leafing through book*) here somewhere.

**TONE** Ran off like he'd lost his mind.　130

**MRS PRESLEY** And you let him, Mr Young?

**MR YOUNG** I assure you, as soon as Sam fled we followed.

**LEE** Ran like the clappers. But we'd no light.

**GABZ** We kept yelling Sam's name. But it just echoed back. It was horrible.　135

**LEE** Voices sounded like they were calling Sam's name from every room.

**MEL** No way! That must have been horrible.

*A pause.*

**MR YOUNG** We only managed to find our own exit by chance. I knew I had to bring up the rest of the –　140

**JOE** (*feebly*) Milton Street Massive.

**MR YOUNG** I hoped that –

**GABZ** – Sam would be …

*A pause.*

**MRS PRESLEY** Well, he's not. (*aside*) As you can see, Rupert. 145

**MR YOUNG** (*aside*) Thank you, Morag.

> *A pause. Mrs Presley and Mr Young look at each other.*

**MRS PRESLEY** Right. I'm calling the police.

**DEZ** (*holds out his mobile*) Miss? Look. Gotta good signal.

**MRS PRESLEY** (*looking at her mobile*) Mine's fine again too. 150 (*starts to dial and pauses*) By the way, where *is* our fake guide?

**MEL** *Who* is she, more like?

**LEE** Yeah. How come she hasn't come back up?

**DEZ** Er, and does that not mean she's still down 155 there with … (*glances at his mobile*) People, is this for real?

**GORDON** Ah, here we go …

> *As Gordon reads, the pupils and Mr Young cluster round Dez. One by one, they express shock, horror and disbelief at the image they see on his phone.*

**GORDON** *'Over the years, many exorcisms were carried out in one of the isolation cells in the basement of* 160 *the city asylum. This was because inmates kept reporting that a hideous, sneering male face appeared on the brickwork and whispered to them …'*

**JOE** Hey, when did Sam hold up that guide 165 woman's light?

DEZ  And pose for my camera with that insane look on his face?

TONE  He never.

GABZ  He was grinning all cheesy when you took    170
your photo, Dez.

JACKY  Looking at me.

GABZ  Whatever, Jacks. Not looking like that anyway.

LEE  Dur! But he's holding the lantern there.

MEL  Staring right out of the picture.    175

GABZ  Not dressed like Sully, even. And his hair's longer.

JACKY  And his eyes are crazed, man.

LEE  Popping.

TONE  Insane.    180

JOE  But that's Sully all right.

GORDON  '… *Unfortunately asylum records show that any inmate who saw this face lost his or her wits completely. Many behaved for the rest of their lives as if possessed by a demon or evil spirit …*'    185

GABZ  Doesn't look one bit like himself.

LEE  When d'you take this again, Dez?

DEZ  Remember that first chamber?

TONE  Where I passed my test.

DEZ  Remember I snapped that fake guide woman?    190

JOE  Then Elvis nabbed your mobile.

GORDON  '… *Records also show that many of these unfortunate inmates …*'

| | | |
|---|---|---|
| **NAT** | How come *she's* not in your photo? | |
| **TONE** | Elvis *is* there. | 195 |
| **GORDON** | ' … *repeatedly tried to escape* …' | |
| **NAT AND DONZ** | The fake *guide*! | |
| **JACKY AND GABZ** | Hey, she's not in that photo right enough. | |
| **MR YOUNG** | I say! | |
| **DEZ** | How come? I definitely took her. | 200 |
| **MEL AND MR YOUNG** | She should be. | |
| **JOE** | Considering she was in that first room. | |
| **TONE** | Holding her light. | |
| **DONZ** | Freaking us out. | |
| **GORDON** | ' … *from the satanic whisperings they kept hearing from the lips of the "Devil's Face" on the wall of their cell. Many took their own lives* … '/ | 205 |
| **MR YOUNG** | /(*interrupting Gordon*) Have you just read that people commit *suicide* after being in that room we've just left? | 210 |
| ***DONZ** | Oh, Sir! | |
| ***GABZ** | That's so gross. | |
| ***JACKY** | Sick. | |
| ***MEL** | Really sad. | |
| ***MR YOUNG** | Appalling. | 215 |
| ***LEE AND TONE** | Yeah. | |
| ***JOE** | Freaky. | |
| ***NAT** | (*shudders*) Ugh! | |
| **MRS PRESLEY** | The police are coming. | |

**GORDON** (*to Mr Young*) Apparently so. If they think they    220
see this 'Devil's Face'. Fruitcakes to begin with,
mind you, poor souls. (*reads on*) ' … *or forced
their way out of the isolation cell …*'

**TONE** Whassat?

**MR YOUNG** Saying that any poor chap –    225

**GORDON** – Or female … I know that when one of the
vaults down there was opened they found
a woman's skeleton. All twisted up, it was.
Dressed in rags. Feet still crossed in chains
from the asylum, although she must have    230
died in one of the rooms closer to the bottom
of that hatch.

**MEL** Like where we started the tour?

**DEZ** And I took my picture?

**MR YOUNG** So anyone who saw the Devil's Face tried to    235
run away.

**GABZ, JACKY AND JOE** Like Sully.

**GORDON** Says so here. (*reads*) '*It is believed that many
of these unfortunate lunatics wandered the
endless tunnels and sewers and passages*    240
*beneath the city …*'

**LEE** Where we were.

**GORDON** (*reads*) ' … *until hunger, thirst or fear claimed
their sanity and their lives …*'

*An approaching police siren is heard and a
silence descends in the office, all attention
drawn to the floor hatch. Suddenly a few loud,*

*slow knocks come from the inside of it. Everyone in the office freezes and looks at the hatch. The knocking continues.*

**DONZ** Miss! 245

**GABZ AND JOE** Sam?

*Mr Young, Joe and Gabz rush to the hatch and Mr Young tries to yank it open. The knocking continues: slow, steady, loud. Mr Young kneels and starts to work the bolt open.*

**GORDON** Sir, I'm not authorised to let you –

**MR YOUNG** Don't worry, Sam! Keep calm. Have you out in no time.

**GABZ** D'you hear that, Sam? Shout if hear us. 250

**GORDON** Sir, I really can't let you –

**JOE** Sam? You listening, mate?

*The knocking continues. Louder.*

**DEZ** Why's he not answering?

**MRS PRESLEY** Come on, Rupert.

**MR YOUNG** The bolt's completely rusted. It won't budge. 255

**NAT** Come on, Sir!

**JACKY** Wiggle it harder.

**MR YOUNG** It's so stiff.

**JOE** You can do it, Sir.

*Joe kneels down and helps Mr Young.*

**NAT, JACKY, GABZ, LEE AND TONE** Come on, Sir! 260

**DONZ** It's working.

MRS PRESLEY Well done, Mr Young. You too, Joe.

MR YOUNG Here we go. Hang on, Sam. You can stop
knocking now. We hear you.

*But the knocking persists as Mr Young slides the
bolt and reaches to raise the hatch.*

MR YOUNG Out you come.                                         265

MEL Wait!

NAT We can't wait.

MRS PRESLEY Of course we can't wait! Let the boy out, Rupert!

*Mel stands on the hatch.*

MEL How do you know that's Sam on the other
side?                                                         270

JOE Easy. (*pause*) SAM!

MEL How d'you know it's not someone else trying
to escape?

*The knocking continues.*

MEL No answer, eh? Could be that guide.

DONZ Miss!                                                     275

GABZ (*calls*) Sully!

DONZ Or one of those …

NAT O-M-G. Dead people.

DONZ Miss!

TONE Dead loonies.                                             280

JACKY (*calls*) That's you at the hatch innit, babes? Say
something. For me, babes.

LEE D'you really think Sam would keep knocking
this long?

JOE  Always up for a joke, our Sully.     285

DEZ  Is anyone laughing at this one?

MR YOUNG  Sam certainly won't be if he's behind that hatch and we won't let him out. He must be terrified.

MRS PRESLEY  Yes. Let the boy out, Rupert.

MEL  Are you sure?     290

NAT  Mel's right. What if it's not him?

GABZ  Move your carcass, Mel.

MEL  Or what if it *is* him.

MRS PRESLEY  Of course it's Sam. Off the hatch, girl!

MEL  But what if it *is* him but he's possessed?     295

DONZ  Miss!

MEL  With the devil?

LEE, TONE AND DEZ  Sam? It that you?

GABZ, JACKY, NAT, DEZ AND JOE  Sam?

JACKY  Move your carcass, Mel. Mrs Presley said.     300

JOE  And open sesame.

*The knocking continues as Mr Young begins to raise the hatch and everyone stares into the hole to –*

DONZ  Miss!

*Blackout.*

*Curtain.*

# The City Below

## By Christopher Edge

**Strange stories hidden beneath great cities**

As you walk down the street, do you ever think about what might be hiding beneath your feet? London, Paris and New York are huge cities that buzz with life above ground. However, beneath their streets and sidewalks lie hidden worlds and strange mysteries.

## London Underground

The London Underground is the world's oldest underground railway and also one of the busiest. Each year more than one billion passengers travel on Tube trains beneath the city. There are 276 stations on a Tube map – from Acton Town to Woodside Park. However, if you look out of the window of a London Tube train, you might spot other ghost stations hidden in the darkness.

Ghost stations are underground stations that aren't used any more. Some of these stations were closed down due to lack of passengers. Other ghost stations have been replaced by newer Tube stops. The empty stations are now thick with dust, but some passengers still haunt their platforms – ghosts!

Here are some ghostly stops on the London Underground:

- **British Museum**: The ghost of an ancient Egyptian mummy was said to haunt this station. After the British Museum Underground station was closed in 1933, two women disappeared one night from the next station along the line. The police who were searching for them found strange marks on the walls of the deserted Tube station. However, the women themselves were never found. Did the ghost take them?

- **Aldwych**: This Tube station was closed in 1994. However, some of the workers who keep the station clean say that a ghostly figure appears on the train tracks at night. She is supposed to be the ghost of an actress. People say she is looking for the theatre that was knocked down to make way for Aldwych Tube station.

- **Farringdon Street**: This Tube station was haunted by a screaming spirit, the ghost of a young girl named Anne Naylor, who was murdered in 1758. When Farringdon Street Tube station closed, the ghost moved to the new Farringdon station. Some say her screams can still be heard on the platforms there today.

### Down Street

During the Second World War, the ghost station at Down Street was used as an air-raid shelter by the Prime Minister, Winston Churchill.

## Down with the Dead Men

Paris, the capital city of France, is famous for many things: its cafés and markets, the Eiffel Tower and Disneyland Paris. But have you heard about the skeletons of the dead that lie beneath the city's streets? To find these frightening bones you will have to enter the Catacombs of Paris.

The Catacombs are a maze of underground tunnels. These tunnels stretch for miles beneath the streets. They are home to the skeletons of six million people. The skulls and bones are stacked in piles. The walls of the tunnels are lined with the skeletons of the dead – a very spooky kind of wallpaper!

So, how did the skeletons end up here?

- In the 18th century, all the cemeteries in the centre of Paris were overflowing. There was no room left to bury the dead.
- New cemeteries were built on the edge of the city. The old cemeteries in the centre of the city were closed down.
- The dead bodies from the old city centre cemeteries were dug up. They were taken down into the Catacombs.
- It took over seventy years for all the skeletons to be laid to rest underground.

Until 2009, the Catacombs were visited by thousands of tourists every year. However, only a short stretch of the tunnels were kept open to the public. Beyond the floodlit tunnels, the piles of bones stretched into the darkness. If you listened carefully, some people said you could hear the moans of the dead begging to go back to the city cemeteries.

**Wartime tunnels**

When Paris was occupied by the Germans during the Second World War, the Catacombs were used as the headquarters of the French Resistance. The French Resistance were fighters who wanted to defeat the Germans. However, the German army also used the Catacombs as an underground bunker to shelter from bombs. It's a good job they never bumped into each other!

**The Mole People of New York**

Movies and TV shows such as *Friends* and *Spider-Man* show the exciting side of life in New York City. However, the city does have some darker secrets. Beneath its streets live the Mole People.

The Mole People is the name given to the homeless people who live in the old sewers and subway tunnels beneath New York City. They make their home among the rubbish and the rats.

Life underground is hard.

- To get electricity, homeless people risk death by hooking up to the electric wires that run through the tunnels.

- They leave the tunnels to steal food from restaurant bins above ground.

- There is no clean water underground – only the rain that floods the tunnels in a storm.

- Every few weeks, the police try to clear the homeless out of the tunnels. Mole People who want to stay in the tunnels have to hide to escape arrest.

It's hard to see why anyone would want to live in such an awful place. However many homeless people feel safer in the tunnels than living on the streets above ground.

**Mole People Myths**

There are many wild rumours about the Mole People.

- They never come above the ground to see the sun.
- They all have grey skin and saucer-shaped eyes.
- They will kill and eat anyone who enters the tunnels.

None of these urban legends is true!

We would like to thank the following schools and students for all their help in developing and trialling *Chamber of Nothing*:

**Little Heath School, Reading**

Luke Carpenter, Jay Carter, Jamie Thompson, Lauren Wallace, Maryam Dim, William Frank, Kai Hammond, Josh Midgley, Charlotte Minton, Ify Ibe, Cameron Love, Ellie Hutchins, Joe Ruchpaul, Ross McAllister

**Portslade Community College, Brighton**